T0328992

Facilitating Rapid Process Improvement Workshops

Facilitating Rapid Process Improvement Workshops

**The Self-Study Guide
for Lean Leaders**

by Sheilah P. O'Brien, MPA, GBLSS, PMA

Routledge
Taylor & Francis Group

A PRODUCTIVITY PRESS BOOK

First published 2021
by Routledge
600 Broken Sound Parkway #300, Boca Raton FL, 33487

and by Routledge
2 Park Square, Milton Park, Abingdon, Oxon, OX14 4RN

Routledge is an imprint of the Taylor & Francis Group, an informa business

© 2021 Sheilah O'Brien

ISBN: 978-0-367-72468-9 (hbk)
ISBN: 978-0-367-72467-2 (pbk)
ISBN: 978-1-003-15490-7 (ebk)

Typeset in ITC Garamond Std
by SPi Global, India

Contents

Preface

As one facilitator to another, we've often been taught our first professional lessons by experts, both in-house trainers and outside consultants. When the training ends, and the consultants leave, we are left to practice our new craft on our own.

Soon, these lessons wear thin. We have gained more experience, but not enough to fill the gaps in our knowledge. Gaps that appear more often.

This manual is written to enhance your knowledge. It is filled with teachings and coaching from someone who has been in your shoes.

It's meant to short cut the time you would take to learn all this on your own.

Acknowledgements

To Brittany Sale, for her tireless assistance in the preparation of this manuscript.

To Jill Turner, for her editing expertise and fearsome support.

To Pitzer College and Cornell University for providing me with a stellar education.

Introduction

Why the Creation of This Manual?

Facilitating Rapid Process Improvement (RPI) Workshops is tough work. The early facilitation training that you received, helped you master the mechanics of Lean and facilitation. But now you have more questions, such as "How do I anticipate the critical junctures/decision points in the workshop?", "Do I know how much data the team needs to collect?" and "What do I do if the sponsor wants to shorten the workshop?"

Contained within this manual, are answers and nuances you may have been missing. It presents a model to know what needs to be done and when to do it!

Organization of This Manual

The chapters are sequenced to match a workshop agenda. Each chapter has its own table of contents and an appendix for handouts and self-study. There are no suggested PowerPoint presentations. You will use flipcharts, examples, and activities to make a point. Activities will come with instructions. The content in the chapter specifies what to say in your own words, when to write on the flip chart, and where to read aloud from examples of 'real-life' RPI's.

How to Use This as a Real Guide

<u>Please take the time to read.</u> There are paragraphs that give you context and background. There are examples of successfully-completed Rapid Process Improvement Workshops (RPI's) that show you how it is done. And the chapter appendix has Self-Study items for more information.

<u>Give yourself time to think as you study the manual.</u> The facilitator-to-facilitator notes will help. They are written in italics and are within parentheses ( ) and look like this: *(Note: these facilitator-to-facilitator notes contain information that perhaps no one taught you; or they contain the important nuances that you sensed, but couldn't put into words.)*

What Is New and Different?

The workshop is divided into two manageable parts for the improvement work ahead. First, making improvements in the process by removing steps that are not necessary, i.e., considered "waste"; and second, making improvements in how the work moves through the process so there are no delays and mistakes. Another difference is the emphasis on data. The team is taught approaches to data collection and coached on the importance of data in support of their improvement recommendations.

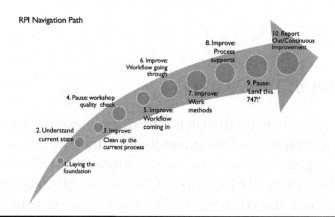

Figure 0.1   RPI pathway

P.S. For a great resource on the fundamentals of Lean thinking, I recommend *Everything I Learned About Lean, I learned in the First Grade* by Robert Martichenko (Lean Enterprise Institute, 2012).

References

Examples and Lessons Taken from Successfully Completed Rapid Process Improvement (RPI) Workshops

Adoptions Process Coos County – RPI
Agency Travel Authorization Process – RPI
Archives Warehouse Storage Process – RPI
Child Welfare Case Transfer Process – RPI
County Health Clinic Patient Processes – RPI
County/State Partners Administrative Processes – RPI
East Metro Food Stamp Intake Process – RPI
Emergency Medical Services Certification Process – RPI
Field Offices Administrative Processes – RPI
Field Offices Client Application Process – RPI
Financial Services Budgetary Process – RPI
Financial Services Receipting Process – RPI
Foster Care Certification Process – RPI
Hospital Patients Transitioning to Community Services Process – RPI
Human Resources Personnel Action Process – RPI
Medicaid Provider Enrollment Process – RPI
Metro Food Stamp Processing Center Application Process – RPI
New Employee Add, Modify, Delete Process – RPI
North Valley Processing Center Applications Process – RPI
OHP Ombudsman Call Processes – RPI
Older Americans Act Allocation Process – RPI
Oregon Health Plan Processing Center Application Process – RPI
Oregon Nursing Board Accreditation Process – RPI
Payroll Timekeeping Process – RPI
Public Health Out-of-State Travel Process – RPI
Vocational Rehabilitation Office Daily Management System
Youth Authority Incident Resolution Process – RPI

Chapter 1

Laying the Foundation

Welcome and Team Introductions

<u>Say in your own words:</u> Welcome. You are participating in a Rapid Process Improvement (RPI) workshop. A RPI can be called a Kaizen event, an Accelerated Change Process, or a Blitz. The workshop is made up of a small team of staff. It occurs over 2–5 consecutive days and is guided by a trained facilitator. The focus of the team is to fix broken processes so they may become Lean processes. This means that the services or products that come out of the process are delivered on time, and without mistakes. (Note: as you go through the manual, make sure you look at each chapter appendix to see what handouts need to be copied to be distributed to the team.)

Team Introductions

Now, let us get to introductions. Please say your name, your working title, and what you do every day. *(This sharing is the first part of building a team.)*

Review "What Is a Process"

(INSTRUCTIONS: Draw a simple process flow flipchart.)

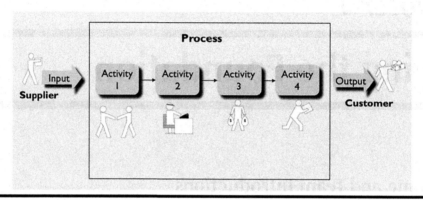

Figure 1.1 Simple process

Say in your own words: Let's review what a process is. See the flipchart. Most people do their work so automatically that they do not realize it has a structure to it. Their work consists of one-time tasks, but mostly the work is made up of routine processes. A process has a supplier, input, process activities, output, and a customer. It is important that you remember this, especially the customer part. *(Many times the team may not be clear about exactly what defines a process. Help them out by saying, "it is repetitive, not just a one-time task. And is made up of sequential step-to-step activities.")*

Learning Process Thinking

Say in your own words: Now we are going to do a roleplaying exercise to get us started. I need a volunteer to play one role while I play the other. (INSTRUCTIONS: Make a copy of the Handout Icebreaker from Appendix 1. Give the volunteer a copy and keep one for yourself. Stand in front of the team and begin reading aloud the facilitator part; the volunteer reading the team member part. The role-play ends.)

Facilitator (F): Please tell the group your job title and the *main thing* that you do in your job. I want you to think about what you do that is repetitive, not just one-time tasks.

Team member (TM): My job title is "provider data entry clerk" and the main thing I do is sit at the computer all day and key in information from filled-out forms.

F: That's great. Let me help you think about this in terms of a process. Remember, I said there was a beginning to a process? The "thing" that begins your work is a form. We call that the input. And I said that something comes out at the end of the process and we call this an output. The output is delivered to the customer.

Now let me ask you an other question: do you know who your customer is?

TM: We don't have customers!

Figure 1.2 Exercise: Icebreaker role play partial

<u>Say in your own words:</u> Let's discuss this exercise. Note the dialogue around the customer. The worker did not think he had any customers. He needs to. If we do not know who our customer is and what they want from our process, it is difficult to know what to improve. Why? Because what we think is a successful output may not be what they requested or expected in the first place. Any comments on the exercise?

Review Preliminary Flowchart

<u>Ask:</u> "Please take out the preliminary flowchart from your packets (this is a flowchart from the specific process(es) that will be the focus of the RPI). Have this in front of you when we meet with the sponsor." *(You will have made up packets for all team members prior to the workshop. Refer to the Addendum.)*

Sponsor Expectations

(INSTRUCTIONS: You have invited the sponsor to come speak to the team. He/she stands in front of the team to explain the expectations of the RPI workshop and answer any questions the team may have. *[You will have coached the sponsor beforehand: the sponsor welcomes the team and expresses appreciation for their time and effort. The sponsor gives background on the problem and what he/she expects from the team's work, saying, "please reach the targets for the goals."])*

How the Rapid Process Improvement (RPI) Came About

Systems and Processes Are Linked

(INSTRUCTIONS: Draw Figure 1.3 on the flipchart.)

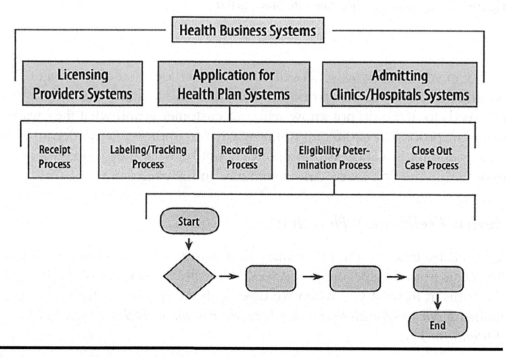

Figure 1.3 Health Systems map

Say in your own words: A sponsor of an RPI is selected after a long series of decisions. Many ideas for RPI's start at the systems/strategic (business systems) level but cascade down to where the work is being done at the detailed process level. It's important to know that what you do at the detailed process level, is to implement the strategies decided at the top of the organization.

Look at the flipchart. The bottom shapes represent the process with its detailed steps. It branches out from the Eligibility Determination process group of the organization. The Eligibility Determination process group is part of the larger Application for Health Plan Systems; one of three systems within Health Business at the top of the chart.

Collecting Data About Problem Areas

(INSTRUCTIONS: Draw Figure 1.4 on the flipchart)

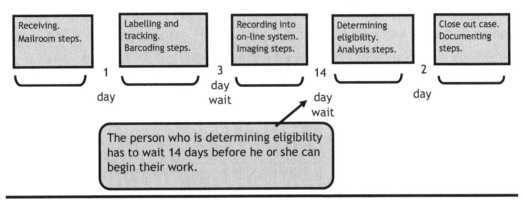

Figure 1.4   Oregon Health Plan (OHP) Processing Center RPI

Say in your own words: Let's drill down another level in this Health Systems Map. As you look at the flipchart, I drew more detail of the Eligibility Determination process group. These are the macro processes that a worker goes through to determine eligibility. A time study was conducted on this workflow to determine whether there were delays. Delays would indicate an opportunity for improvement and become a focus for the RPI team. Note the delay of 14 days between the 3rd and 4th boxes (different macro processes). The team would begin their work by asking "why is there such a delay, why is this happening?" Once they answer that, they will determine what detailed process they need to analyze.

(There can be some confusion about the differences and use of Value Stream Maps (VSM) and process maps/flowcharts. VSMs are to be "big picture." They are to give a picture of flow of "product/service development, from concept to launch" or "fulfillment from order to delivery." Each rectangle shape is a macro process on the VSM and represents many detailed processes. Here's the difference: one of the detailed processes is flowcharted is from the time of supplier input to the output delivered to the customer.)

Background and Charter

Review Information Packets

<u>Ask</u>: the team to take out the rest of the material from their information packets. *(You will have prepared these packets ahead of the workshop. Refer to the Addendum.)*

(INSTRUCTIONS: The charter will be included in this packet but saved for review until last. Point out one pertinent thing about each document. Documents are regulations, findings from audits and evaluations, news stories, websites, organization charts, position descriptions, a list of IT systems, software, and desktop applications.

Go over any other data that have been collected about the process thus far, and tell the team we will go over the charter last. Answer questions.)

Review Charter

<u>Say in your own words:</u> Ask the team to look at the charter from their packet. Explain to them that "this is the contract we have with the sponsor." Have them read it. Answer questions.

(If need be, ask the sponsor to return to the team room to provide clarification on the charter.)

<u>Say in your own words:</u> Note the goals/baseline measures on that charter. We take baseline measures of how the process is performing before the RPI begins. After improvements are implemented, we take the same kind of measures that we took in the baseline. At the end of the RPI, we compare the before and after measures. The comparison shows the percentage of improvement which ties to the goals of the workshop. *(There can be confusion about the words "metric" and "measure." For example, measures are the cycle times before and after improvements. The metric is the calculation from the comparison of the two measures. Usually, these are expressed as a percentage.)*

<u>Say:</u> Here is a handout with more detail.

Team Leader	Becky D.		Facilitator	Paddy O'Brien
	Name			**Unit**
Team Members	Bonnie R.			Proc. Ctr., Mgr.
	Ellen R.			OHP Proc. Ctr.
	Michelle B.			Payroll
	Robin D.			CAF Field
	Laer H.			OIS
	Sharon M.			Payroll
	Cam F.			Human Resources
	Debbie G.			OSH - Food Services
Sponsor	Shawn J.			
Problem Definition	Nothing adversely affects employee morale more than problems with their pay. "Locking time" is a function performed by managers who are responsible to review, validate, and approve "time worked" that is inputted into the system by the employees the manager is responsible for. Employees are responsible to check their available leave hours before they request it. Over ¼ of all DHS employees (2500) have not had their time locked by their managers every month. As a result, employees are not paid on time; staff expends time in corrections and expediting special payments. In addition, there are grievances filed by employees that must be resolved and there are BOLI violations that must also be resolved.			
Scope	The scope will involve the analysis and subsequent streamlining to the 'locking time' process. This will begin with Payroll verifying if the OSPS Leave Accrual Reports are used and submitted to supervisory managers and end when the employee is paid correctly. (Sub-processes: Requesting and Inputting Time, Assuring employees are paid, Processing Timesheets, Correcting Timesheets.)			
Objectives	To improve and standardize a process for time locking that ensures that all DHS employees are paid accurately and timely. To develop future state reports that will meet customer needs.			
Timeframe	Planning: June 18-July 27 Conduct: August 20,21,22 Follow up: August 23, Sept.1			
Baseline Data	• 10,752 corrections a year. • 3336 special checks a year.			

Figure 1.5 Payroll Timekeeping RPI Payroll Charter

Goals for the Workshop

- Reduction of time sheet corrections by 50% within 60 days and 100% in 6 months and $0.
  Baseline measure: 10,752 corrections a year.
  Baseline measure: Staff time: $18,000 a year.

- Reduction of issue of special checks by 50% in 60 days.
  Baseline measure: 3336 checks a year.
  Baseline data: Cost of check ($50): $166,800 a year.

- Eliminate paper time sheet distribution and processing.
  Baseline measure: 120,000 timesheets a year.
  Baseline measure: Staff time: $107,775 a year.
  Baseline measure: Hummingbird system: $4000 a year.
  Baseline measure: Mail and distribution: $10,800 a year.

- Eliminate the need to process overpayments.
  Baseline measure: 720 overpayments a year.
  Baseline measure: Staff time: $81,000 a year.

- Increase the collection or resolution of current overpayments:
  Baseline measure: $62,000 YTD needed to be collected.

- Decrease employee grievances. (The team noted that this may initially increase then decrease.)
  Baseline measure: 18 grievances a year.
  Baseline measure: Staff time and fees: $27,000 a year.

- Reduce time and errors in the local office process:
  Baseline measure: Employee process steps: 13; Handoffs: 3
  Manager/supervisor steps: 5; Handoffs: 3
  Baseline measure: 20% error rate

- Reduce time in the central office and OSPS process:
  Baseline measure: Process steps: 53 steps; Handoffs: 14

Figure 1.6   Example: Administrative Services Payroll Timekeeping RPI Goals/ Baseline Measures

(If you look at the Goals for the Workshop example, note that there are other baseline measures collected, not just the ones pertaining to the customer who expects accuracy, i.e., time sheet corrections. This is noted by the goal "Reduce time and errors…" These other measures are the number of outputs, volume of work and hand-off data.)

Tracking Collection of Baseline Data

<u>Say in your own words:</u> There will be times when you take on an RPI assignment, and discover early that there are no baseline data. You need to start collecting it right away. (This is noted in the Addendum, prep work for the RPI.)

Here is a good form to use to document the details of any data collected.

(INSTRUCTIONS: Draw the example of the first column on the PHD Metrics form below.)

Metric #	PHD01.1_4 (Assigned from PMO
Metric Label	Rework
Definition	Percentage of travel authorizations requiring rework (e.g. documents/information is missing or inaccurate
Calculation	Number of requests returned to originator for correction dividedby total requests in the same period.
Type:	Workload Metric? Service Cycle Metric? Quality? People? Circle the metric that best identifies the type.
Source	OOS Travel Tracker
Data Owner	Travel Coordinator
Data Frequency	Weekly
Baseline	75% (10/02/15 touch time survey)
Target	25%
Target timeline	3/01/16
Benchmark utilized	None

Source: Public Health RPI

Figure 1.7 Example: Public Health Out of State Travel RPI metrics definitions

<u>Say:</u> This is an excellent example of good labels and definitions for tracking your information about metrics. *(This is an invaluable tool for the team to use. Many times, people can challenge the RPI team as to how they collected the data. This tool also ensures consistency when collecting measures post-RPI.)*

Say in your own words: What if it is impossible to collect real baseline data? You can turn to industry benchmarks to give you a good alternative.

(INSTRUCTIONS: Read aloud: "When you do not have your own base-line measures, you can go to benchmarking resources. Pick an industry or another state government. Benchmarking is a technique in which a company measures its performance against that of best in class companies, determines how those companies achieved their performance levels, and uses the information to improve its own performance. Subjects that can be benchmarked include strategies, operations and processes." (ReVelle, 2014, pp. 8–9))

Ground Rules and Decision-Making

Team Develops the Ground Rules

Say in your own words: There are a couple of self-governing tasks we need to complete: rules and decision-making. Every workshop team needs to have its own rules of how they want to operate.

(INSTRUCTIONS: Draw Figure 1.8)

Examples of rules

- Arrive on time each day of workshop
- Respect all ideas
- Hold judgement until time to make decisions
- Help out if behind schedule

Figure 1.8   Workshop rules

Ask: "As you look at this flipchart, do any of you want to change these items or add to them?" *(Record answers on flipchart and post on wall.)* "Does everyone agree?"

Team Determines How to Make Decisions

(INSTRUCTIONS: Draw various decision-making models, Figure 1.9)

> **Examples of decision-making**
> • Majority rules
> • Consensus building

Figure 1.9   Decision-making models

Say in your own words: As a team, how are you going to make a decision? Let me explain the meaning of each model on this flipchart. (For example, "Consensus basically means 'give and take.'")

(INSTRUCTIONS: Facilitate a discussion to get the team to all agree on what decision model they are going to use. And record this on the flipchart. *Here is an example of an adopted model: "We would emphasize collaboration and use consensus for important decisions and issues. For less important issues, we will rely on the subject matter expert.")*

Administrative Tasks

Documentation

(By the time this part of the workshop comes around, the team may think things are going pretty slooooow. I sense this and tell them, "Be patient. We start slow so we can go faster.")

Say in your own words: Soon we will be doing some "real work." We will be out in the physical place where the process work occurs. You will be interviewing staff, examining files, and drawing charts. Since we do a lot of our work quickly, we will track it by making notes or copying forms. All of this work will be put into our Workpapers Notebook.

(INSTRUCTIONS: As the team does their work, you will need to coach them about what to ask for regarding documentation, e.g., requesting a copy of a blank form. They should be coached to only take copies of filled-out forms (that may have to be redacted), spreadsheets, etc. *[Remind the team to write a citation at the bottom of the page they collect that includes date, the source of the document, and their initials.])*

Keeping Track of Improvement Ideas

Say in your own words: Not only do we not want to lose the work we accomplish, we also do not want to lose any improvement idea, however big or small, developed or undeveloped. Throughout the workshop, improvement ideas will pop up at any time. We won't stop the agenda to respond to them, we will just quietly capture them on a Plan, Do, Study, Act Form.

(INSTRUCTIONS: Hand out the Plan, Do, Study, Act PDSA form, and the Completed PDSA Form, OHP Processing Center RPI Mailroom PDSA form from Appendix 1.)

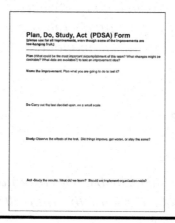

Figure 1.10   Blank PDSA form

Figure 1.11   Example: PDSA form Oregon Health Plan Processing Center RPI, pg.1

> **What we did was... (Brief description of the activities)**
> Paul pulled out fifty applications from the OHP trays, ran them through the "slitting machine", took them to his desk, opened each envelope, assembled the application, date stamped it, scanned all applications with labels. He then input the information for the apps with no labels, printed the labels and matched to the applications. The applications were then ready to be assigned to workers.
>
> **Study:**
>
> **What happened was ... (the results, data)**
> Paul has able to complete the entire process described above in two hours.
> In a separate step fifty applications were assigned to eligibility workers. The total time for assigning applications was seven minutes.
>
> **Looking at what happened we learned that ... (lessons learned)**
> We learned that by eliminating wait time, sorting and employing continuous flow methodology we were able to get an OHP application into the hands of an eligibility worker in less than three hours instead of the 24-30 hours under our current process.
>
> **Act:**
> **What we plan to do next is ... (state changes that will be made to test in the next cycle)**
> We would like to test the continuous flow of the application through the eligibility completion. (See proposal to test new work flow.)

Figure 1.12 PDSA form OHP, Processing Center Application Process RPI pg.2

<u>Say in your own words:</u> How many of you know what the scientific method is? Basically, it's collecting enough data to support a point. Collecting data to run a test to either prove or disprove a hypothesis. This is foundational to an RPI's success. I use the Plan, Do, Study, Act method to test a new idea. Fill out this PDSA form for your improvement ideas. *(Sometimes, teams get stuck in their thinking on how to fill out a PDSA form, so I give them a tool that is used to develop a finding in internal auditing. I tell them to think about what they want to write by referring to these categories:* **Condition** *(what is the problem/issue? What is happening?),* **Effect** *(So what? Why should anyone care about the condition? What is the impact?),* **Cause** *(How or why did the condition occur? (We may have to use the cause and effect diagram to get here.)* **Criteria** *(What is the way it should be according to law, policy) and* **Conclusion** *(After all this, what is to be done?)*

Any time, before, during, and after the workshop day, you can take a PDSA form from the blank forms tray and fill it out. And put it in the filled-out forms file tray. At a minimum, fill out the "Plan" section. (See Addendum for prep for the RPI.)

Data Collections Methods

<u>Say in your own words:</u> Collecting data can be daunting. With any improvement idea, if we do <u>not</u> have data to support our recommendations, they will not be accepted by the sponsor. Let's review what is doable during this RPI.

(INSTRUCTIONS: Hand out Data Approaches from Appendix 1.)

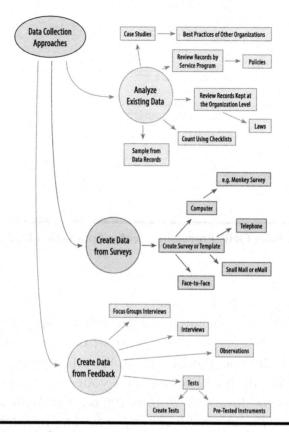

Figure 1.13   Data Approaches
Source: O'Brien, 2017, pp. 8–9.

Please look at your handout. It describes data collection approaches. From left to right on the chart, there are branches. The first thing you ask yourself is, "do the data exist?" *(I have worked in organizations that do not have the needed data. So the team had to collect it or ask for the sponsor's assistance to collect it.)* If they don't exist, there are two branches to follow, "create data from surveys" and "create data from feedback." And if it does exist, you move to the "existing data" branch.

Also, as part of my approach, I add the seven quality tools to enhance data analysis. The tools are cause and effect diagram, check sheet, control chart, histogram, pareto chart, scatter diagram, and flowcharting. Some of these you will use in this workshop.

(These data collection approaches coupled with the seven quality tools are manageable by the RPI team. Because small improvements, one after

another, are the essence of the RPI workshop, simple data collection is appropriate and easy to use. This is what is displayed on the data approaches map using analysis tools such as check sheets, tracking time sheets or small non-statistical sampling. Simple data should not be over-analyzed, it should be used to point the way to next steps. For example, many RPI teams don't know how big a sample should be. You, as the facilitator, are safe to suggest a non-statistical sample size of 20, where every fifth document is pulled from a universe of 100.)

The Art of Facilitation: Review Each Day

At this point, the team is still very dependent on you to facilitate. Soon, they will become more self-sufficient.

At the end of the day, after the team has left the workshop room, study the work that has been recorded or noted on flipchart paper. As you read the flipchart notes, look for emerging ideas for improvement. Do some sorting and resorting of ideas that appear similar and create a new list of potential improvement opportunities for the team to see on Day 2.

Whatever else is on the remaining flipcharts, "do something" with them: synthesize and rewrite them for you own facilitation notes or move them to a flipchart marked "Parking Lot" to be addressed later in the workshop.

During the workshop, the team may need additional data. They can gather it themselves or request someone outside the team (who is a data expert) to collect it for them. When the data documents arrive, make copies for the team and ask one person to summarize the data. Record this on a flipchart titled, "Data, Day 1", etc., to discuss.

Next, reflect on how the team is doing. Is there someone on the team who is being left out, left behind, or exhibits any resistance to the activities? Don't let time pass; visit privately with that team member early on Day 2. Also, review what leaders may be emerging from the team. They will take on a more prominent role during the workshop, as you, the facilitator, move more and more to the background.

One final note to remember. The team will go down rabbit holes or veer off the road. From the beginning, help the team to understand the customer's needs and requirements. This is pivotal to facilitating. Many times you will need to redirect the team by asking the question, "Who is your customer?" This helps bring the team back into focus.

List of facilitation deliverables

■ Big picture map (body of work chart or value stream map).
■ Customer-to-quality tool results.
■ Product family chart.
■ Team decision of ground rules.
■ Team decision of what decision-making model to use.

Appendix 1

SELF-STUDY: Classification system of processes
    As a reminder, list of materials in background packets: examples

■ RPI Agenda.
■ Charter.
■ Excerpt from Ways and Means Legislative presentation that includes this process (or some document that details information about the organization or program).
■ Preliminary flowchart.
■ Pertinent laws or policies that affect the process.
■ General data about the process.
■ Organization chart.
■ Findings from any audits.
■ Position descriptions.
■ IT system and software.

SELF-STUDY: Process classification
    The American Productivity Center has done a lot of work for us. They have developed a hierarchy of processes that takes all the guessing out. Use this when needing help in identifying and naming a process in your own organization.

HANDOUT: Icebreaker (This handout does not go to the whole team, but only to those who have a role in the icebreaker.)

Facilitator (F): Please tell the group your job title and the *main thing* that you do in your job. I want you to think about what you do that is repetitive, not just one-time tasks.

Team member (TM): My job title is "provider data entry clerk" and the main thing I do is sit at the computer all day and key in information from filled-out forms.

F: That's great. Let me help you think about this in terms of a process. Remember, I said there was a beginning to a process? The "thing" that begins your work is a form. We call that the input. And I said that something comes out at the end of the process and we call this an output. The output is delivered to the customer.

Now let me ask you an other question: do you know who your customer is?

TM: We don't have customers!

F: Ah, but you do. The term "customer" is something we are not used to. Think of it as the person who receives your work. For a doctor, the customer would be the patient. For a teacher, it would be a student.

TM: Oh, right. I do the data keying and it comes out on a report that prints off somewhere else and then another person works with that report.

F: Then that person is your customer. That report is the output. That is the "thing" that is produced after you finish all your activities.

TM: You know, I do this every day and sometimes I wonder, is what I do worth it to anyone?

F: That is a great question we should all ask. How does what we do every day fit into the big picture? To help you see how your work aligns with the big picture, let's go through a "so-that chain." Start with the first thing you do in your work and then add "so that" and then move to the next thing you do and add "so that." This is repeated until you reach the end of the process.

TM: I key in data *so that* new healthcare doctors, hospitals, and clinics are registered *so that* they can be paid to provide care to our clients *so that* our clients have access to healthcare treatment. Wow, I do that?

F: And you said you didn't know whether what you did every day was worth it to someone. From your data entry work to a client getting treatment, that is a big contribution.

Figure 1.14   Full page icebreaker

HANDOUT: Goals and Baseline Measures; Payroll Timekeeping RPI.

Goals for the Workshop

- Reduction of time sheet corrections by 50% within 60 days and 100% in 6 monthsand $0.
  Baseline measure: 10,752 corrections a year.
  Baseline measure: Staff time: $18,000 a year.

- Reduction of issue of special checks by 50% in 60 days.
  Baseline measure: 3336 checks a year.
  Baseline data: Cost of check ($50): $166,800 a year.

- Eliminate paper time sheet distribution and processing.
  Baseline measure: 120,000 timesheets a year.
  Baseline measure: Staff time: $107,775 a year.
  Baseline measure: Hummingbird system: $4000 a year.
  Baseline measure: Mail and distribution: $10,800 a year.

- Eliminate the need to process overpayments.
  Baseline measure: 720 overpayments a year.
  Baseline measure: Staff time: $81,000 a year.

- Increase the collection or resolution of current overpayments:
  Baseline measure: $62,000 YTD needed to be collected.

- Decrease employee grievances. (The team noted that this may initially increase then decrease.)
  Baseline measure: 18 grievances a year.
  Baseline measure: Staff time and fees: $27,000 a year.

- Reduce time and errors in the local office process:
  Baseline measure: Employee process steps: 13; Handoffs: 3
  Manager/supervisor steps: 5; Handoffs: 3
  Baseline measure: 20% error rate

- Reduce time in the central office and OSPS process:
  Baseline measure: Process steps: 53 steps; Handoffs: 14

Figure 1.15 Goals for Payroll Timekeeping RPI workshop full version

HANDOUT: PDSA Form

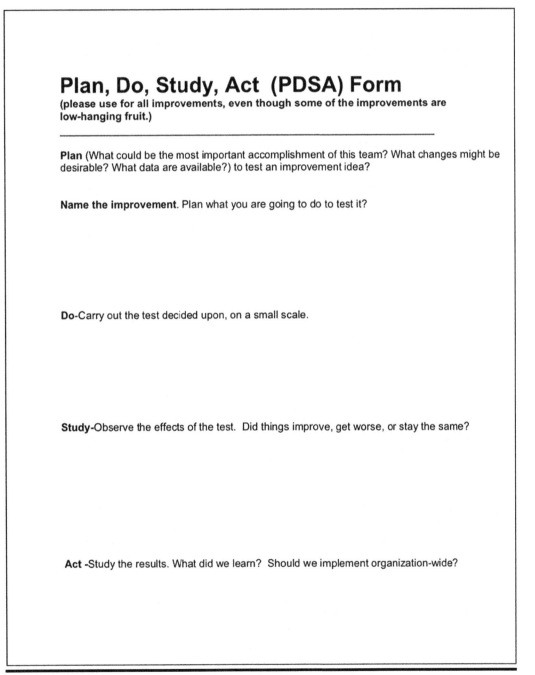

Plan, Do, Study, Act (PDSA) Form
(please use for all improvements, even though some of the improvements are low-hanging fruit.)

Plan (What could be the most important accomplishment of this team? What changes might be desirable? What data are available?) to test an improvement idea?

Name the improvement. Plan what you are going to do to test it?

Do-Carry out the test decided upon, on a small scale.

Study-Observe the effects of the test. Did things improve, get worse, or stay the same?

Act -Study the results. What did we learn? Should we implement organization-wide?

Figure 1.16   Blank PDSA forms

HANDOUT: Completed PDSA form-OHP Processing Center

Project Team: Rapid Process Improvement	Report Date: July 14
Improvement Strategy addressed in this cycle: Eliminate wait time and sorting done in mailroom/bar coding	

Cycle open/scan make labels	Cycle Begin Date: 06/14	Cycle Completion Date: 06/14

Plan:
<u>What</u> we plan to do… (State the basic plan) **Fifty applications will be taken from OHP trays as soon as they are received in the mailroom. The person testing, who will be Paul, will run the fifty applications through the "slitting" machine and take to his desk to start the opening and labeling process.** **Paul will open each envelope, staple the application and any other documents, date stamp the application and scan any with labels. The applications with no labels will be set aside. Paul will then make the labels for those applications and, print the labels and attach to the applications. At this point applications could be immediately assigned to workers.** <u>Who</u> **will do this?** Paul <u>When</u> **will this be done?** June 14 beginning at 7:30 a.m. <u>Where</u> **will this be done?** In the OHP mailroom
In order to … (tie it back to the aim) The current opening/bar coding process takes two days. The applications are opened, date stamped, and assembled by the mailroom staff. The mailroom staff sorts the applications by teams. The next day the applications are sorted again by teams, news and reapps, scanables/non-scanables, language, and priority applications. The bar coding staff then begins scanning the applications with labels. Then they make labels for the applications with no labels, attach the labels, and deliver the applications to the Case Setup area.
Prediction: (What we think will happen…) We think that we can drastically reduce the amount of time it will take to get an OHP application into the hands of an eligibility worker, by reducing wait time, unnecessary sorting, and establishing a continuous flow.
Do:

Figure 1.17   OHP PDSA, pg.1

What we did was… (Brief description of the activities)
Paul pulled out fifty applications from the OHP trays, ran them through the "slitting machine", took them to his desk, opened each envelope, assembled the application, date stamped it, scanned all applications with labels. He then input the information for the apps with no labels, printed the labels and matched to the applications. The applications were then ready to be assigned to workers.

Study:

What happened was … (the results, data)
Paul has able to complete the entire process described above in two hours.
In a separate step fifty applications were assigned to eligibility workers. The total time for assigning applications was seven minutes.

Looking at what happened we learned that … (lessons learned)

We learned that by eliminating wait time, sorting and employing continuous flow methodology we were able to get an OHP application into the hands of an eligibility worker in less than three hours instead of the 24-30 hours under our current process.

Act:

What we plan to do next is … (state changes that will be made to test in the next cycle)

We would like to test the continuous flow of the application through the eligibility completion. (See proposal to test new work flow.)

Figure 1.17   OHP PDSA, pg.2   (continued)

HANDOUT: Data Collection Approaches

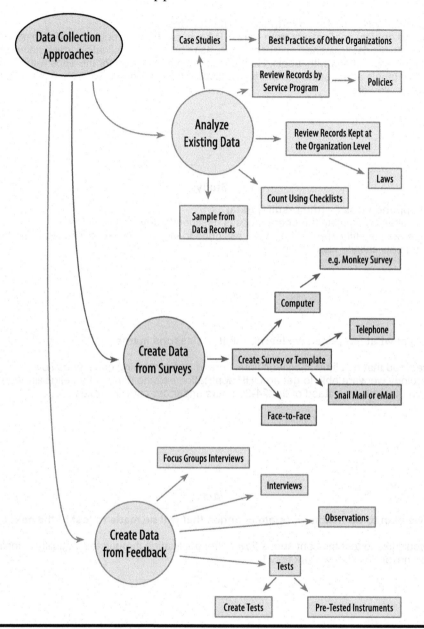

Figure 1.18   Data Collection

PCF ID	Hierarchy ID	Name	Difference Index	Change details	Metrics available?
20025	5.0	**Deliver Services**	67	+20026, +20040, +20058, NEW	Y
20026	5.1	Establish service delivery governance and strategies	14	+20027, +20032, NEW	N
20027	5.1.1	Establish service delivery governance	5	+20028, +20029, +20030, +20031, NEW	N
20028	5.1.1.1	Set up and maintain service delivery governance and management system	1	NEW	N
20029	5.1.1.2	Manage service delivery performance	1	NEW	N
20030	5.1.1.3	Manage service delivery development and direction	1	NEW	N
20031	5.1.1.4	Solicit feedback from customer on service delivery satisfaction	1	NEW	N
20032	5.1.2	Develop service delivery strategies	8	+20033, +20034, +20035, +20036, +20037, +20038, +20039, NEW	N
20033	5.1.2.1	Define service delivery goals	1	NEW	N
20034	5.1.2.2	Define labor policies	1	NEW	N
20035	5.1.2.3	Evaluate resource availability	1	NEW	N
20036	5.1.2.4	Define service delivery network and supply constraints	1	NEW	N
20037	5.1.2.5	Define service delivery process	1	NEW	N
20038	5.1.2.6	Review and validate service delivery procedures	1	NEW	N
20039	5.1.2.7	Define service delivery workplace layout and infrastructure	1	NEW	N
20040	5.2	Manage service delivery resources	25	+20041, +20050, +12127, NEW	N
20041	5.2.1	Manage service delivery resource demand	9	+20042, +20043, +20044, +20045, +20046, +20047, +20048, +20049, NEW	N
20042	5.2.1.1	Monitor pipeline	1	NEW	N
20043	5.2.1.2	Develop baseline forecasts	1	NEW	N
20044	5.2.1.3	Collaborate with customers	1	NEW	N
20045	5.2.1.4	Develop consensus forecast	1	NEW	N
20046	5.2.1.5	Determine availability of skills to deliver on current and forecast customer orders	1	NEW	N
20047	5.2.1.6	Monitor activity against forecast and revise forecast	1	NEW	N
20048	5.2.1.7	Evaluate and revise forecasting approach	1	NEW	N
20049	5.2.1.8	Measure forecast accuracy	1	NEW	N
20050	5.2.2	Create and manage resource plan	7	+20051, +20052, +20053, +20054, +20055, +20056, NEW	N
20051	5.2.2.1	Define and manage skills taxonomy	1	NEW	N
20052	5.2.2.2	Create resource plan	1	NEW	N
20053	5.2.2.3	Match resource demand with capacity, skills, and capabilities	1	NEW	N

Figure 1.19   Example of city government processes (Source: APQC, n.d.)

References

APQC. "Process Classification Framework." American Productivity and Quality Center, n.d. http://www.apqc.org/pcf (accessed 05/31/20).

ReVelle, Jack B. *Quality Essentials: A Reference Guide from A to Z*. Milwaukee: ASQ Quality Press, 2014.

O'Brien, S.P. *Lean for the Nonprofit: What You Don't Know Can Cost You*. Portland, OR: Inkwater Press, 2017.

Chapter 2

Understand the Current State

Walk Through the Actual Place of Work to Grasp the Big Picture

<u>Say in your own words:</u> A process described in a charter does not replace seeing the process in its physical layout and observing the people doing the work.

We will be taking two different tours of the workplace; the first to get the big picture, the value stream. The second will be of the specific process we are to improve. (Remind them that we covered the difference between a value stream and process flowchart.)

(You, as the facilitator make the arrangements for the team to be escorted by a member of the staff to get a walking "tour" of the big picture, and then a tour through the detailed process. If the team is too large, they may have to be broken up into smaller groups of 2–3 people.)

<u>Say in your own words:</u> I will give you little instruction for this activity, other than to take a notepad. Just some guidance; remember you are in someone else's workspace. Try to be as unobtrusive as possible. (INSTRUCTIONS: When the team is finished with their tour, and return to the team room, capture reactions and observations and write on the whiteboard available.)

(WHAT IF? *What if it is not possible to get a tour of the physical layout and see the work? The facilitator then arranges for a "surrogate tour." A supervisor or lead worker who has an intimate knowledge of the big picture, meets with the team and takes them through the tour verbally. The supervisor* *can provide visuals such as a PowerPoint presentation or present a mind map, or engage in roleplaying as if they are the "piece of paper" going through the process.)*

> *"It was interesting for me to follow the application process and imagine it was a person. First, we date stamp your forehead, put a name tag on you and then throw you in a drawer for 20 days..."*
>
> - Sharon, RPI Team

Figure 2.1   From a member of the team for the OHP Processing Center Application Process RPI

Receiving. (mailroom steps)	Labelling and tracking. (barcoding steps)	Recording in online system. (imaging steps)	Determining eligibility. (analysis steps)	Case closing (documenting steps)

Figure 2.2   Example: OHP Processing Center Application Process RPI Value Stream/ macro view

Here is where the walk-through occurred:

Figure 2.3   Mailroom photo

This is a photo of the walk-through of the OHP Processing Center beginning in the mailroom...and then moving on to the labelling/tracking section called the Case Setup Area. One RPI team member decided to sketch out the floor plan of the Case Set Up Area showing where staff sat and where different file systems were located. The team member noted the movement and frequency of the staff to different filing systems. This is a good example of extra information picked up during the walk-through.

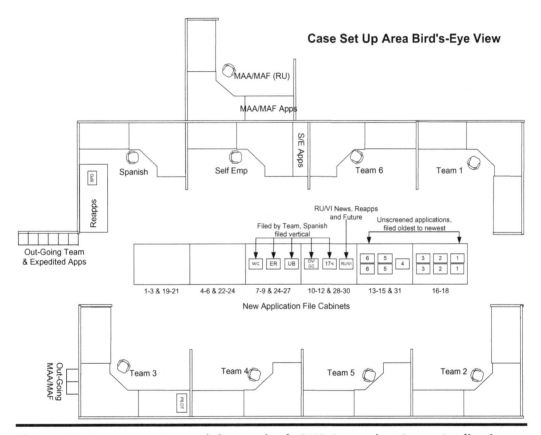

Figure 2.4 How case set-up unit is organized, OHP Processing Center Application Process RPI

In the Older Americans Act Allocation Process RPI walk-through, the team was made aware of timelines that affected the flow of work. They decided to capture these deadlines to provide more of the big picture.

	Feb/March	July 1st	Oct 1st	Feb/March	June 30th	July 1st	Oct 1st	Feb/March
Fed FY		25% FFY 1		100% FFY 2				75% FFY 3
State FY			SFY 1				SFY 2	
	1st allocation		2nd allocation	3rd allocation			4th allocation	5th allocation

1st allocation:	Final prior biennium allocations & planning allocations for upcoming biennium (includes updated funding formula for demographic changes)
2nd allocation:	Finalize budget changes following the end of the legislative session, finalize NSIP allocations and revise for III B, C-1 & C-2 transfers
3rd allocation:	Final allocations for SFY 1 and revised planning allocations for SFY 2
4th allocation:	Finalize NSIP allocations and revise for III B, C-1 & C-2 transfers
5th allocation:	Final allocations for the biennium and planning allocations for next biennium

Figure 2.5   Example: Older Americans Act (OAA) Allocation Process RPI, due dates for submitting documents

After the walk-through of the Metro Food Stamp Processing Center, the RPI team created a picture of their impressions of what they saw.

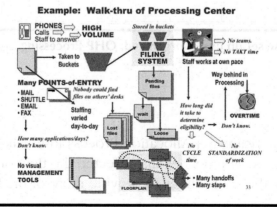

Figure 2.6   A picture of what RPI team saw walking through the Metro Food Stamps processing center

The Second Walk-Through: Specifically of the Process to Be Improved

<u>Say in your own words:</u> The goal of this walk-through is to get a clear picture of the specific process(es) that the RPI team will work on.

Materials needed for the walk -through:

- A clipboard

- Graph paper for drawing

- Notepaper to record interviews

- Blank forms to fill out a Handoff
  Chart and a Spaghetti Diagram

Figure 2.7   Materials needed for walkthrough

(INSTRUCTIONS: Hand out Instructions: Walk-through of the current process, to all the team from Appendix 2.)

<u>Ask</u> the team to read the instructions. Answer any questions they may have.

**HANDOUT: Instructions: Walk-Through the Process
to Be Improved (partial)**

Your walk - through will likely use a "talk-through" as a method for cognitive tasks in that you cannot observe these activities being performed. Much of the talk-through may occur as you map the work processes, especially if you do a thorough job in documenting the knowledge that guides decision-making…

Figure 2.8   Walk-through instructions partial

(In Chapter 1, we went through the information packet. Make sure the team has looked at the preliminary specific process(es) flowchart from the packet. They will be creating a new flowchart from information off the preliminary flowchart and from any new information they gathered on the walk-through.)

<u>Say in your own words:</u> There are a lot of activities in this walk-through. You will gather information as you walk through the work area. I need all

of you to sign up for a mini-group of 2–3 people that will separate out the work that needs to be done back in the team room.

One group is going to draw a spaghetti chart that shows the traffic path of the workers in the process. Another group will draw a handoff chart. This is a round circle graph that shows the points where the document going through the process is handed off to the next workstation. Another team will look at a floor plan of the work area and denote where there are faxes, printers, and copiers, as well as intact work groups. (These are people who routinely work together.) And the last mini-group will focus on building on the preliminary flowchart to create a new flowchart.

These are explained more in the instructions that I will be handing out to each mini-group.

HANDOUT: Instructions: The Spaghetti Chart

Spaghetti charts are used to identify waste of time and resources in work paths. They are prepared as a scaled map of the work floor on a standard worksheet (a piece of graph paper)...

Figure 2.9   Handout spaghetti chart partial

HANDOUT: Instruction: The Handoff Chart (Partial)

The approach is to start with a circle representing the world of the process. Each function is reprinted on the circle as a point on the circumference...

Figure 2.10   Handout instructions handoff partial

(INSTRUCTIONS: Tell the team where each mini-group will meet. Specify areas of the team room or other nearby rooms. Then begin to meet with each group.

Before meeting with the floor plan mini-group, obtain a blueprint from the work area from the sponsor. Instruct them to mark up the floor plan noting where faxes, printers, copiers, and storage areas are located. After they gather information from the walk-through and return to their meeting place, give the team 60–90 minutes to do their work.

Next, meet with the handoff and spaghetti charts mini-groups. Hand out the instructions for a spaghetti chart and instructions for a handoff chart from Appendix 2. Go over instructions and demonstrate how to do each chart. After they gather information from the walk-through and return to their meeting place, give the team 60–90 minutes to do their work.)

(Many times, a team doesn't understand the need to focus on handoffs. It is important to reiterate, that every time there is a handoff, there is room for something to "fall through the cracks." When a handoff is made, the document could sit idle in someone's In Box or it could be placed in an unfamiliar place, lost for a long time. All this stalls the process; and costs money.)

(INSTRUCTIONS: Meet with the preliminary flowchart team. Have them retrieve the preliminary flowchart from their packets. Have ready a stack of graph paper to hand out.)

<u>Say in your own words:</u> I am going to give you instructions for the creation of an accurate flowchart. Here they are: We need to update the preliminary flowchart. Your goal is to come back from this second walk-through with information to develop an accurate picture of the process. Use the preliminary flowchart merely as a guide. Look at it to get a "lay of the land" but then put it aside. Start fresh and draw a new flowchart (on the graph paper provided) using your notes, forms, and sketches from the walk-through. Remind the team that all decision points and loopbacks should be put on the chart. (INSTRUCTIONS: Provide materials and suggestions of how they can display their new flowchart: options are large pieces of blank newsprint with a supply of blank sticky notes nearby. Or work with a sticky wall which is a solid-colored plastic tablecloth that has been fully sprayed with spray glue on one side. The tablecloth is taped to the wall with the sticky side showing. Supply ½ sheets of 8 × 10 paper to represent steps of the process.)

Give them 60–90 to complete their task.

(The Time Observation Form is included in Appendix 2 if you want to hand it out.)

Time Observation Form

			Process:
			Observer:
			Date:

Step	Activity	1	2	3	4	5	6	7	8	9	10	11	12	Shortest Repeatable	Comments
Cycle Time															

Figure 2.11 Time observation form. Example: Another way to collect data on a walk-through

Analysis of Data, Observations from Walk-Through

(INSTRUCTIONS: When the mini-teams return to the team room and complete their tasks, ask them to display their work so the whole team can see it. Tell them that they will to the rest of the team on their observations and conclusions.)

Say in your own words: Let's start with the **handoffs**. Please display your handoff chart on the wall and give us a summary. *(For this purpose, the team will only have one handoff chart, the "before" picture as displayed below on the left side of the example schematic. After the RPI, they will have an "after" handoff chart.)*

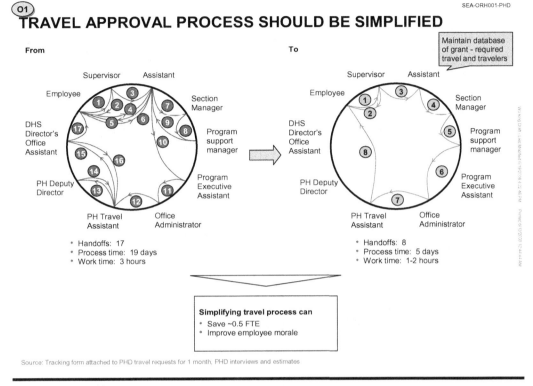

Figure 2.12   Example: Hand-off charts, Public Health Out of State Travel RPI

(INSTRUCTIONS: After the handoff summary ends, read aloud the Public Health Director Quote.)

> Frances K., Director of Public Health in Klamath County, created a handoff chart of the process she has togo through to request a budget amendment from the County Board of Commissioners. When she took it to the next board meeting, the board became aware of how complex the whole process was and vowed to change it.
>
> - Partners RPI

Figure 2.13   Example: This is from the County/State Partners Administrative Processes RPI. How a County Public Health Director used a handoff chart to get her budget passed!

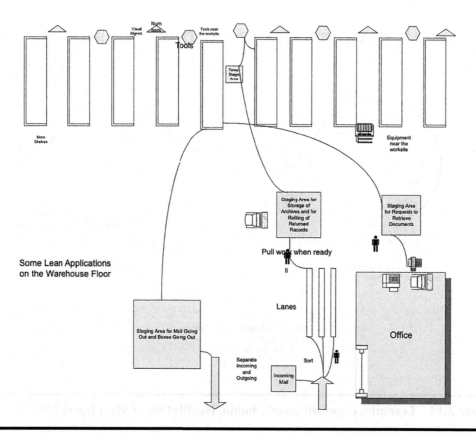

Figure 2.14 Example: The Archives Building floorplan. Tools should be near where the work is being done

Say in your own words: Now who got a blueprint or a **floor plan** and was able to mark it up? Please display it and summarize where all the fax machines, printers, and copiers are located. Also, point out if there are formal staff work teams or informal, such as individuals who work with each other on a daily basis. Where are they located on the floor plan? *(Note that the example of the floorplan was used also to trace the travel paths of the staff. Again, as with handoffs, the team may be wondering why they are* *doing this task. Explain that when machines and people are placed far from where the work needs to be done, it takes more time to get the work done. Time is wasted in moving from one place to another and that costs money.)*

(INSTRUCTIONS: Record on a flipchart any observations added by the rest of the team.) 📊

<u>Ask</u> the team to listen to an example of how a walk-through resulted in gathering enough information that this RPI team could document costs. (INSTRUCTIONS: Read aloud Figure 2.15.)

Example from Walk-through Analysis, East Metro Food Stamp Intake Process RPI

"For example, to walk from the furthest case manager's cubicle to the furthest ops manager's cubicle required 98 steps and took 1 minute. Walking from the furthest case manager's cubicle to reception took 139 steps and 1 minute 24 seconds. Note, however, that I walk quickly, with long steps (I'm tall) and no one stopped me with a question. Compare these times to no steps required and roughly zero seconds to send an instant message. Assuming a person sitting at the far end of the building may have to go to reception 5 times in one day, 5 * 2 (round trip) * 1:24 = 14 minutes per day in travel time alone. Assuming 200 work days per year, this results in a savings of 46.67 hours per year spent walking back and forth to reception. At approximately \$16/hour, this represents \$746.72 wasted each year per worker. Since branch 3501 has approximately 50 workers, the branch is spending \$37,336 by not implementing Group-wise Instant Messenger."

- Derek S. RPI Team Member

Figure 2.15   Example: Metro Food Stamp Intake Process RPI from walk-through analysis

<u>Say in your own words:</u> Whoever did the spaghetti diagram, please display it and tell the team what you observed.

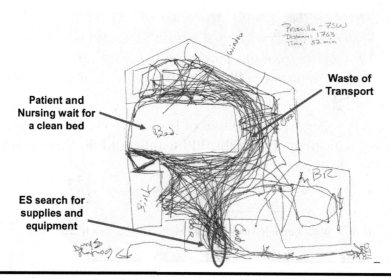

Figure 2.16 Oregon Public Managers Association. Example: Spaghetti chart of preparing a hospital room

(A spaghetti diagram looks like a bowl of overflowing spaghetti that shows that convoluted work paths take time; and resources that may not be necessary. Areas on the spaghetti chart where work paths look jumbled are areas which need to be realigned and reorganized. The solution is to identify ways to redesign the flow to reduce unnecessary movement of people and materials. These opportunities will be addressed in the next set of improvements on "smoothing out the flow.")

Backlog

Backlog is a problem in many organizations. (Invariably, while on the walk-through, someone will discover that there is a backlog of work. Backlog is when the work has piled up and the organization cannot get caught up. If backlogs are not eliminated, any improvement work can quickly come undone.)

Figure 2.17   Backlog

(Although cleaning up the backlog is not a responsibility of the RPI team, it does affect you as the facilitator. You need to bring it to the attention of the sponsor. The sponsor may seek your advice on what to do. You will need to advise the sponsor that a plan for backlog should be developed quickly and implemented. The handling of the backlog should be a separate workload from the day to day work done in the targeted process. Some organizations choose to handle this by approving overtime for the daytime workers or by hiring temps. In any case, advise the sponsor to determine the extent of the backlog and what it would take to clear it up. Here are some examples of determining the extent the backlog that can be shared with the sponsor. Also see the Self-Study on backlog in Appendix 2.)

BUCKETS	BACKLOG
Form 223-REDETERMINATIONS	18 days out
Form 15-859 A's	8 days out
Form 504-Changes and miscellaneous	25 days out

In lieu of a formal tracking system, the RPI team hand -counted the number of documents in each bucket to get a count of volume of backlog. (This did not include the work that had just been taken from the buckets and distributed to other SDA 3 Field Offices for help in processing.)

           - North Valley Processing Center RPI

Figure 2.18   Example: Backlog Tally, North Valley Processing Center RPI

Backlog summary

Number of workers   17

Remaining backlog

Day	Recert	Medical	852	853	APR	943	Ret. Pend	Other
Baseline	400	331	226	55	46	16	38	135
6-Oct	375	317	219	55	42	14	34	127
7-Oct	338	308	194	52	37	13	30	109
8-Oct	303	291	178	50	34	12	24	81
9-Oct	273	267	160	45	30	11	14	56
10-Oct	249	247	138	41	28	10	3	34
13-Oct	234	233	132	38	27	7	0	25
14-Oct	224	228	125	35	25	7	0	7
15-Oct	213	219	112	29	25	7	0	0
16-Oct	211	204	110	15	25	7	0	0
17-Oct	211	204	110	15	25	7	0	0

Completed backlog

Day	Recert	Medical	852	853	APR	943	Ret. Pend	Other
6-Oct	25	14	7	0	4	2	4	8
7-Oct	37	9	25	3	5	1	4	18
8-Oct	35	17	16	2	3	1	6	28
9-Oct	30	24	18	5	4	1	10	25
10-Oct	24	20	22	4	2	1	11	22
13-Oct	15	14	6	3	1	3	3	9
14-Oct	10	5	7	3	2	0	0	18
15-Oct	11	9	13	6	0	0	0	7
16-Oct	2	15	2	14	0	0	0	0
17-Oct								

Figure 2.19 Example: Backlog data Medicaid Provider Enrollment Process RPI

Backlog Plan

1. Determine the amount of the backlog

2. Determine the average cycle time of processing one application or request. (<u>Five time</u> observations of low and high-end performers, then averaged.)

3. Divide cycle time into available minutes per day for

Figure 2.20 Backlog plan partial

Revise Preliminary Flowchart

<u>Say in your own words:</u> Will the mini-team for the new flowchart please display it on the wall next to the old (called preliminary) flowchart?

(INSTRUCTIONS: Sometime during a break make sure a large replica of the preliminary flowchart is displayed on the wall. Next to it will be a space and blank surface for the revised flowchart to be displayed.)

<u>Say in your own words:</u> Now that we have reviewed the work of the handoff chart, spaghetti chart, and the floorplan mini-groups, I want all of us to hear from the new flowchart mini-group. As you listen, if there is anything that you think is missing or not quite right, write it on a sticky note and put it up on the flowchart in the location of the process where it applies. Then after the presentation, we will discuss all sticky notes and make any additional revisions to the chart.

(At this point, there will be lots of activity and discussion until people agree that they have a complete and accurate flowchart. If there is disagreement on the team, send someone back to the observed workplace to seek clarification and return to report to the team.)

Say in your own words: our work if not finished with our new flowchart. (INSTRUCTIONS: As the facilitator, remove the sticky notes from the flowchart and make sure its appearance is clear, i.e., that the process steps and direction lines are clearly defined.)

<u>Say in your own words:</u> Our work is not finished with our new flowchart.

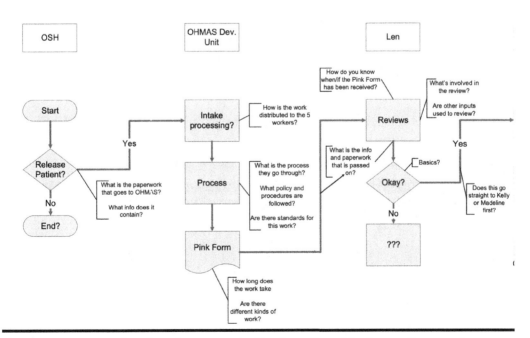

Figure 2.21 Example: Flowchart, Hospital Patients Transitioning to Community Services RPI

Below is an example of an analyzed flowchart. Questions (on sticky notes), will be answered to revise the flowchart.

(INSTRUCTIONS: Ask the team for volunteers to do the following tasks:

- Count the number of tasks and write the count on the flowchart.
- Record the estimated time between the steps and write on the flowchart.
- Record the estimated timeline along bottom of chart of the cycle time (can be a group of steps).
- Write down the number of staff at each 'work station' notated on the flowchart.)

<u>Say in your own words:</u> This completes the "understanding the current state" phase. We have collected a lot of information. If you have any ideas for improvement, however undeveloped, put them on a PDSA form and put in the appropriate file tray. If you have any work that should go into the Workpaper Notebook, please put it there and don't forget to put your name and date on the bottom of the page. As an added note, I have been adding items to the Parking Lot flipchart. Please review it to see if anything needs to be added.

List of Facilitation Deliverables

- Sketch of each team member's process from walk-through or Time Observation Sheets.
- Completed Revised Process map.
- Completed backlog plan for notebook.
- Spaghetti charts with team notes and markups.
- Handoff charts with team notes and markups.

Appendix 2

HANDOUT: Instructions: Walk-Through the Current Process

HANDOUT: Instructions: Walk -Through the Current Process

- Your walk -through will likely use a "talk-through" as a method for capturing cognitive tasks (you cannot observe these activities being performed). Much of the talk-through may occur as you map the work process, especially if you do a thorough job in documenting the knowledge that guides decision-making.

- You will still want to observe the work area in which each task or decision is executed and have a staff person lead you through how he or she moves between tasks. You will want to observe any storage areas that are accessed, computer screens that the performer must work with in doing his or her job.

- Remind yourself that the kinds of waste you will observe in an office work process will usuallyinvolve working with information and especially the paper forms or computer screens that carry information. Frequently these forms or screens are poorly designed so that the sequencing and display of information neither coincides with the flow of work or enables speedy recognition of their contents, thereby causing and wasting valuable time to search. Sometimes forms contain contents that are unnecessary and obscure. Get copies of forms. They can be improved to only include what is necessary. Watch out fo rmoving information from one paper form to another or from a paper form to a computer screen. This is the waste of resources and time in duplication. Watch for staff completing incomplete information that has been given to them or are correcting incorrectinformation. This is the waste of rework. Entering information into multiple software applications because these applications do not "talk to" each other is waste. Again, fix in your mind that for office processes, information is the equivalent of the physical materials used in manufacturing processes.

Figure 2.22   Handout instructions walk-through

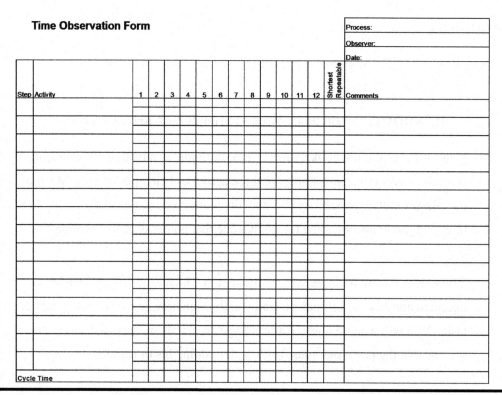

Figure 2.23   Time observation form

HANDOUT: Instructions: Spaghetti Chart

HANDOUT: Instructions: The SpaghettiChart

Spaghetti charts are used to identify waste of time and resources in work paths. They are prepared as a scaled map of the work floor on a standard worksheet (a piece of graph paper).

The procedure for drawing spaghetti charts requires the team member to observe the workflow, identify work points. Work points are the key points on the process map where you can identify work stations/process activities taking place. You will use connecting lines to show the pathway of the work flows from work point to work point.

To start, just observe the workplace. See where the activities happen (work points). Closely observe how the information, material and people move about to accomplish the tasks during an average workday.Once these points have been identified, these points should be marked on a form or just graph paper.

The next step involves detailing how things move with the process, from one point to another. For this, lines can be drawn to link up the work points. Thecompleted chart can look like a bowl of spaghetti when finished. Where work paths look jumbled up; these are areas which need to be realigned and reorganized. Identify ways to redesign the flow to reduce unnecessary movement of people and materials. Assess how many times each processing station is used.

Figure 2.24   Handout instructions Spaghetti chart

HANDOUT: Instructions: The Handoff Chart

HANDOUT: Instructions: The Handoff Chart

The approach is to start with a circle representing the world of the process. Each function is reprinted on the circle as a point on the circumference.

The points should be equally spaced on the circle even if the actual physical locations aren't geographically equidistant.

The process is then traced from the point of entry into the process, and every time there is a change in the functional owner, a lineis place inside the circle linking the 'from' and the 'to'.

For all the handoffs, the total number of types of handoffs and the total volume of handoffs in a given time period are calculated. Each and every handoff is an opportunity, or several opportunities, for mistakes to happen or for something to simply fall through the cracks and never get done. Thus, the goal is to reduce the number of handoffs in the process.

Figure 2.25   Handout instructions for handoff chart

SELF-STUDY: How to calculate how long it will take to clear a backlog
BACKLOG PLAN

Backlog Plan

1. Determine the amount of the backlog

2. Determine the average cycle time of processing one application or request. (Conduct five time observations of low and high-end performers, then averaged.)

3. Divide cycle time into available minutes per day for one person = # of applications that can be processed in one day.

4. Determine how many people are available to do the work.

5. This will give a schedule of how long it will take to clear up the backlog.

Figure 2.26 Backlog plan

Here is an example of a calculation for a backlog plan.

Example: 425 applications in the backlog: all the while new applications are coming.

1. Gather data.
   a. # of pieces of paper (e.g. applications or requests) in the backlog.
2. Measure cycle time for one unit.
   a. Pick both the high producer and the low producer workers in the process. Conduct time observations (at least 5 cycles; then average) of each. Then get an average cycle time from the two workers. (one worker takes 30 minutes average; the other takes 60 minutes average = 45 minutes.) Example: it takes 45 minutes to process one application.
3. Calculation: cycle time for one app=45 minutes. Hours in the workday = 7.6 hours. Convert to minutes (7.5 x 60) = 430 minutes.
4. Number of apps that can be completed in one day by one worker = 9.1 apps. (430/45 = 9.1).
5. Number of days to eliminate current backlog = estimated 46 days (425/9.1 = 46+ days for one person.
6. Want to clear up backlog quicker? Two people can do 18 apps per day (425/18 = estimated 24 days).

Figure 2.27 Example: Backlog Calculation, Medicaid Provider Enrollment RPI

There is a backlog of 425 applications. Simply, you determine how long it takes to process one application. Then you calculate the number of hours available in a day to figure out how many days it will take to eliminate the backlog. And if you want to clear up the backlog quicker it, look at number 6 of the plan. They added another person to the job and cut the time it would take to clear up the backlog.

From these calculations, you could apply them differently: if you are given a deadline for clearing up the backlog, how many people would it take?

Chapter 3

Improve
Clean Up the Current Process

Preparation for Step-by-Step Exercise

(This exercise will use the new flowchart from Chapter 2, to be displayed on the wall.)
    (INSTRUCTIONS: Draw on the flipchart Figures 3.1 and 3.2.)

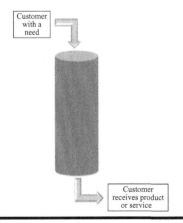

Figure 3.1   A Straightforward Process Flow

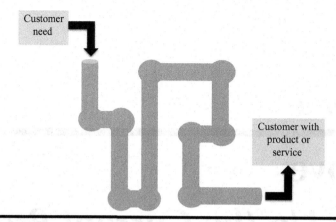

Figure 3.2   A process that has morphed

<u>Say in your own words:</u> From the flipchart, you can see a very simple, clear process. Then the process changes, it "morphs" over time. It turns into this second picture with a lot of bends and twists. These are places where unnecessary activities/waste reside.

(So far, the workshop team has been exposed to laying the foundation. They are anxious to "do something." This "step-by-step exercise" is the first part of making improvements to the process. [The second part is smoothing out the flow.] When completing this exercise, the team will immediately see results of their work.)

<u>Say in your own words:</u> We are going to conduct a step-by-step analysis of the process using our revised flowchart. But first, I want to draw another picture for you.

(INSTRUCTIONS: Draw on the flipchart.)

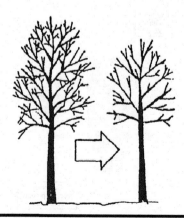

Figure 3.3   Unpruned tree to pruned tree

Think about this picture. When we take waste out of a process, it is much like pruning a tree. Pruning removes the excess branches, and the deadwood to allow room for new growth! You are going to prune the process; label each step on our current flowchart either "value" or "necessary" or "waste."

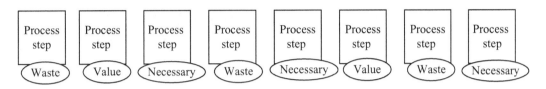

Figure 3.4   Step by step schematic. Labelling each step as to value

(INSTRUCTIONS: Draw on the flipchart the definitions on Figure 3.5 and read aloud the definitions.)

VALUE (Value-add) – activities essential to deliver the service or product to the customer.

NECESSARY – activities that are necessary/required but add no real value from a customer viewpoint.

WASTE – activities that add no value from the customer's perspective and are not required for financial, legal, or business reasons.

Figure 3.5   Definitions for step-by-step

(You will get more questions to clarify "necessary" and "waste." Necessary is a step that has to be done, i.e., it is required by law or policy. "Waste" is harder to explain. Understanding what the customer expects and wants is the key to whether the step in the process is waste or not waste, rather it is valued by the customer. For example, if the price is too high for a product or service [because it includes things the customer didn't expect to pay for], the customer will take their business elsewhere.

But what about government or nonprofits, who do not have traditional customers, who cannot "take their business elsewhere?" How can the RPI team understand waste/no value? I tell the team to ask, "As the product or service moves through the process, does the work task change 'it' in some way to move it closer to its final form? Or does it just sit idle, or even worse, does it get passed on without anyone performing any task on it?" If it physically changes in some way, it has value, otherwise, it is waste or is necessary.)

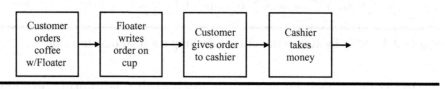

Figure 3.6   Coffee Place before improvement

Conduct Step-by-Step Exercise: Explain the Tool

(INSTRUCTIONS: Hand out Coffee Place Before, Appendix 3.)

<u>Say in your own words:</u> Take a look at this. We all get coffee, right? This example of ordering and getting coffee from a local barista has 30 steps. Can you identify what is a valuable step and not a valuable step? *(Make this informal. If there are comments said loudly, respond to each person about their comment, then move on to the next comment. As always, participation helps build your team.)*

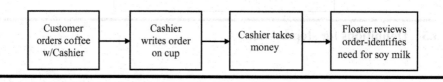

Figure 3.7   Coffee place after improvement

(INSTRUCTIONS: Hand out Coffee Place After, Appendix 3.)

<u>Say in your own words:</u> This handout represents the results after a step-by-step analysis. Take a few minutes to look at both workflows side by side.

ABOUT THE QUESTION	ABOUT THE ANSWER "YES"	ABOUT THE ANSWER "NO"
Note: the whole of the question is to see if the step 'moves' the product or service through' the process to get it to its final form before it is delivered to the customer.	Note: Keeping these steps in the process may suffice for now, but there is more improvement waiting. This step could be	Note: For every step that the answer is 'no'‚ implies removing it. Make sure that if you remove it, that that removal doesn't

Figure 3.8   Step-by-Step tool partial

(INSTRUCTIONS: Hand out the Step-by-Step Analysis tool in Appendix 3.)

Say in your own words: As you read this handout of the tool, it will help you analyze the flowchart by asking certain questions. This tool has columns for the question to ask, the answer, and the appropriate action.

(Make sure there is clarity about the handout. There will probably be questions about loopbacks. Explain that loopbacks can indicate waste and can impede the smooth flow of the process.)

Say in your own words: Before we start the analysis, take a look at the bottom of the step-by-step tool where it shows you a diagram of a loopback. A loopback shows up when a piece of work is returned to the previous step for correction.

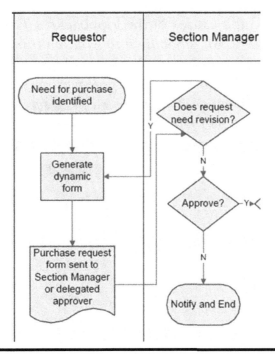

Figure 3.9   Example: Financial Services Receipting Process RPI flowchart partial of loopbacks

Loopbacks on a flowchart can point to errors (however defined) that need to be corrected. "Correcting" adds time and therefore adds costs to the process. If an application is submitted and it "travels" through the workflow and suddenly it is sent back to the previous step, that is a loopback.

There are always errors in any process, but what we are interested in, is the frequency of these errors and the reasons for their occurrences. Are these one-time errors or do they occur more often, and could be a sign of a systemic problem?

(INSTRUCTIONS: Ask for two volunteers who will determine the frequency of the loopback(s) and interview the staff as to the reason for the loopback. This will result in an estimated completion/accuracy rate. Explain that you need to know how many loopbacks are caused by incomplete tasks or that the loopback was necessary because there were errors in what was passed on.)

<u>Say in your own words aloud so the whole team hears:</u> "What these volunteers will do is determine the frequency of the loopback. They will go out to the work floor and find the staff involved in these steps around the loopback. They will ask the staff to give them an estimation of how often this happens in a month (or pick another period of time based on the volume of work of the process, e.g., 3 or 6 months). Then they will probe as to the causes of the loopbacks. *(If this is a small percentage (less than 30%), attribute it to random human error. If it is over 30%, as estimated by the staff, the volunteers will need to investigate further and collect more data. (Other organizations think that 30% is acceptable rework. But no organization wants to see 50% rework.) They will interview staff and get their opinion on the cause(s) of the loopback. They will write this up in notes and bring back to the team room.)*

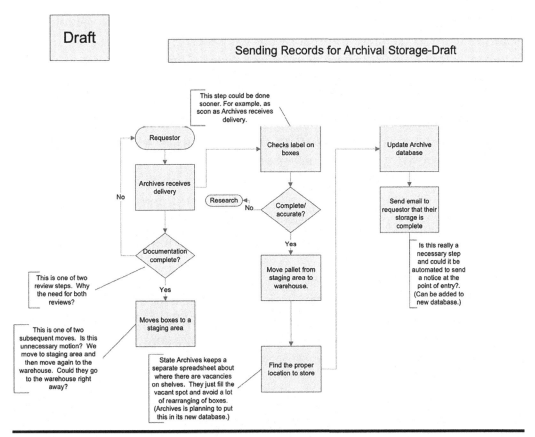

Figure 3.10   Example: questions about the process, Archives RPI

<u>Say in your own words:</u> Let's look at the step-by-step tool and answer the questions for each step.

(INSTRUCTIONS: Stand in front of the flowchart on the wall. Start a general discussion about what steps the team thinks are waste. Mark those steps with a sticky note as "waste." Then start reading aloud the questions from the tool. Begin with the directions on the tool. (This will enable the team to also review the steps that were marked "waste" from the general discussion.) Midway, stop facilitating this exercise and ask for a volunteer from the team to facilitate the rest of the exercise.)

(Your role should be to get the exercise started. Once it gets going, the volunteer facilitator(s) can carry it to its fruition. Remind the team to be "as sure as they can be" when they are selecting what to label each step. This exercise does not need to be overly-complicated. For right now, all you expect in this exercise is to get rid of the steps that all agree are unnessary/waste.)

<u>Say in your own words:</u> We have completed this exercise. The waste steps are removed. I am going to draw an "X" through them.

Earlier, we went through loopbacks and, as you can see, we have a new flowchart that still has some loopbacks. To probe further, we will need to know the root cause. will review the use of root cause tools at the end of this chapter.

I also want to point out the elapsed time between steps in the process. This indicates opportunities for more improvement which will be part of the next part of improvements, "Smoothing out the flow." We collected data on time between steps in Chapter 2. Did we remove some waste during this exercise that would affect the time between steps? If so, by how much?

Teach/Review Root Cause Analysis Tools

<u>TEACHING EXERCISE</u>

(Prepare the team that a change of pace is happening in the workshop. reviewing knowledge about tools. Although they did some initial querying of staff as to the reasons for loopbacks, this interview did not have the rigor of root cause analysis.)

<u>Say in your own words:</u> Remember the importance of finding data to support our improvement recommendations?

How many of you have used root cause tools? How many of you have completed a cause/effect/fishbone diagram or conducted a Five Why's exercise? *(Note the people who have raised their hands. If some of the team need help during the exercises, you can ask the more experienced team members to assist them.)*

(INSTRUCTIONS: Draw on the flipchart Figure 3.11.) 📋

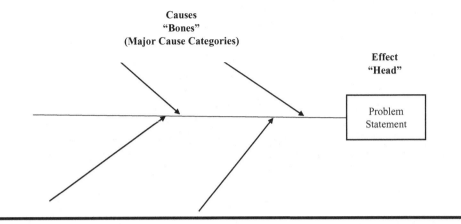

Figure 3.11   Generic cause and effect diagram

Say in your own words: We are going to start with the cause and effect diagram. This diagram is often called a fishbone diagram. The fish head is the problem that we are trying to find the cause for. The body, the fish bones, are the causes of that problem.

We are going to do an exercise: I'll give you the problem and write it on this blank diagram.

(INSTRUCTIONS: Write on the flipchart: "Not all clients who come for appointments can be seen." Assign the team into groups of three and give each mini-team a blank flipchart piece of paper and flipchart pens. Ask them to draw an outline of the fishbone diagram.)

Say in your own words: Here is the context for the problem: People were showing up at a health clinic at the time of their scheduled appointment and had to wait a long time to see their provider. Since many of the clients worked and had limited time or depended on public transportation, many left before their names were called.

Why is this a problem? Not only does the client not get the care he/she came for, but the clinic loses revenue because it receives federal match money based on the number of clients that are seen.

> **Cause and effect diagram**
>
> There are four steps to using this tool.
>
> 1. Identify the problem.
> 2. Work out the major factors involved.
> 3. Identify possible causes
> 4. Analyze your diagram

Figure 3.12   Cause and effect instructions partial

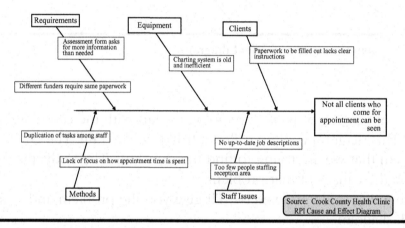

Figure 3.13   County Health Clinic Patient Processes RPI C&E diagram

(INSTRUCTIONS: Hand out instructions for the cause and effect diagram, Appendix 3. Give the team time to read it. Answer any questions.)

Say in your own words: We are going to use our cause and effect instructions to find the cause of the problem on the flipchart. I'll give you 20 minutes for the exercise. *(This is an important exercise that teaches directly "how to do it.")* After you complete your cause and effect diagram, each mini-team will present it to the rest of the group. Anyone can ask questions or make comments.

(INSTRUCTIONS: When all the presentations have been made, hand out the completed County Health Clinic Cause and Effect diagram from Appendix 3. Give the team time to briefly look at it.)

Say: Here is an example from an RPI. This is their completed cause and effect diagram.

(If there is time, you can continue to train them how to use the Five Why's Tool.)

<u>Say in your own words:</u> How many of you have heard of the Five Why's exercise? It is another cause discovery tool. It can be used in a number of ways. I have used it when I have completed a cause and effect diagram and the team has agreed on the primary cause and it is in need of more "drilling down." I use the Five Why's tool to gain more detail about the probable cause or causes.

Here is a fun example of a Five Why's exercise. (INSTRUCTIONS: Read aloud the words from Figure 3.14.)

Messersmith, Donald H. 1993. **Lincoln Memorial Lighting and Midge Study.** *Unpublished report prepared for the National Park Service. CS-2000-1-0014. N.p*

Problem: One of the monuments in Washington D.C. is deteriorating.

Why #1 – Why is the monument deteriorating?
- Because harsh chemicals are frequently used to clean the monument.

Why #2 – Why are harsh chemicals needed?
- To clean off the large number of bird droppings on the monument.

Why #3 – Why are there a large number of bird droppings on the monument?
- Because the large population of spiders in and around the monment are a food source to local birds.

Why #4 – Why is there a large population of spiders in and around the monument?
- Because vast swarms of insects, on which the spiders feed, are drawn to the monument at dusk.

Why #5 – Why are some swarms of insects drawn to the monument at dusk?
- Because the lighting of the monument in the evening attracts the local insects.

Solution: Change how the monument is illuminated in the evening to prevent attraction of swarming insects.

Figure 3.14 This is from a study done by the National Park Service

---

The 5 Whys is a technique used to analyze a problem, and in many cases, it can be completed without a data collection plan.

By repeatedly asking the question "Why" (five is a good rule of thumb), you can peel away the layers of symptoms which can lead to the root cause of a problem.

Figure 3.15 Five Why's instructions partial

(INSTRUCTIONS: Hand out Five-Why's Instructions from Appendix 3.)

Say in your own words: Take a look at the instructions for the Five Why's. Do you have any questions?

(If the team needs you to illustrate another example, take a cause from the cause and effect exercise and record it on the flipchart. Facilitate the team to ask and answer the Five Why's, and record the answers on the flipchart.)

The Workshop Could Stop Here…

(There are many times during the workshop that improvement solutions are obvious, yet, because of the structure of a week-long workshop, those solutions have to wait. But plans can change.)

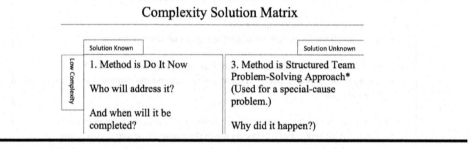

Figure 3.16   Complexity/Solution matrix partial

Say in your own words: Not every process problem requires a weeklong workshop (RPI).

During the course of the workshop, some solutions present themselves sooner than later. Therefore, the workshop may move at a faster rate than expected.

(INSTRUCTIONS: Hand out the Complexity/Solution Matrix from Appendix 3.)

Say in your own words: Here is an example of a matrix that can help decide whether the planned workshop duration should be altered.

The decision is based on two factors: 1. how complex the process is, and 2. whether a solution is already known. Note the different quadrants on the matrix. Pay attention to the corresponding methods and protocols as footnotes. Discuss. *(The team may have their own suggestions to shorten the workshop, but it's ultimately the sponsor who makes the decision. It is time for you, the facilitator, to provide some coaching to the sponsor. Carefully study the Complexity/Solution Matrix [Appendix 3] with the sponsor and see if there is any merit in changing the agenda and perhaps shortening the workshop. Assure the sponsor that as long as the tools, Matrix chart protocols are used for each quadrant, he/she can be confident that the team has collected enough data for the sponsor to make the appropriate decision.*

If the RPI ended at this point, the team would have made significant improvements just by removing waste from the process. They also will have an accurate current flowchart of the process that will be useful in training new employees.)

List of Facilitation Deliverables

- Completed PDSA Forms.
- A revised process map (flowchart).
- Five Why's results.
- List of top three causes for each rework situation.
- Parking lot flipchart.

The Art of Facilitation: What Is Value?

The Lean term, "value" can be tough to understand.

When you are shopping for a new car, you look at the sticker that is displayed on the driver's window. Here, you will find the most basic information about the vehicle, such as make, model, and year. There is also a list of Standard Equipment on the left side and a list of Optional Equipment on the right.

As you look at the new car information, it can include information about factory-installed options (sometimes bundled into packages) as well as options you can pick and choose. Whatever you choose can affect the price of the car.

Imagine a car dealer whose stickers on new cars don't separate out the basic, standard costs from the optional choices, i.e., the "bells and whistles." There is only one price displayed.

Looking at the one price, the buyer thinks he is buying only what is essential to drive a car. When the invoice is presented and broken out into line items, the customers refuses to pay for the extras because he did not choose them. His perceived value of the car only included the basic package, only what is essential to have the car get him from point A to point B. Additional optional features were not considered to have value for the buyer.

Appendix 3

HANDOUTS:

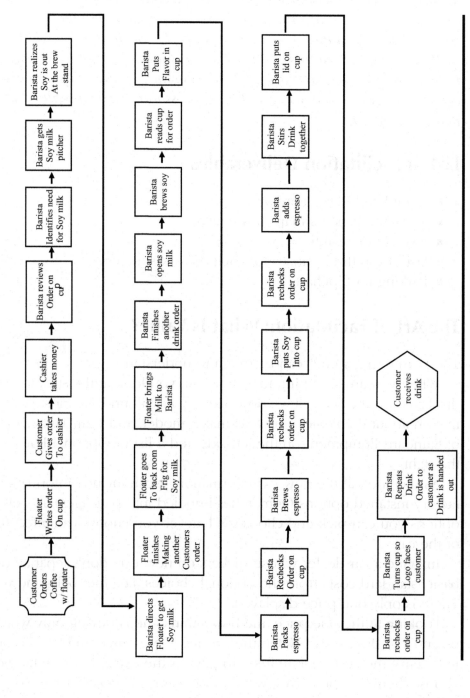

Figure 3.17 Before coffee place

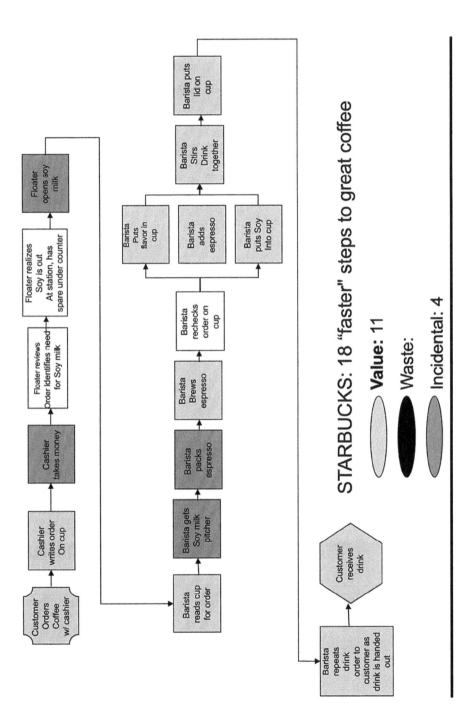

Figure 3.18　After coffee place

ABOUT THE QUESTION	ABOUT THE ANSWER "YES"	ABOUT THE ANSWER "NO"	ABOUT THE ACTION
Note: the whole of the question is to see if the step 'moves' the product or service through' the process to get it to its final form before it is delivered to the customer.	Note: Keeping these steps in the process may suffice for now, but there is more improvement waiting. This step could be moved in its sequence or combined with other steps. For now, all we want is to remove the steps that obviously have no value.	Note: For every step that the answer is "NO"- this implies the step should be removed. Make sure that if you remove it, that nothing else in the process is adversely affected.	Note: Some steps can readily be eliminated; other steps need more investigation. And there are other steps that don't seem very valuable, but are considered necessary, such as required by law.
Question 1: a. Is this step necessary because of a law or regulation? b. Or does this step physically change the product or service going through the process?	a. Keep the step in the process. b. Keep the step in the process.	a. Analyze further the reason the step is necessary. b. Analyze why the step is there.	For example, this means someone 'touched' the document going through the process, i.e. wrote on it or attaching it to something. It didn't just sit idle. The litmus test is to ask, "did this step move the piece of paper closer to the final form it should be? If no, these are probably steps labelled 'file' or 'pend', etc. If so, then our process is not moving toward the ideal, or the process would have continuous flow and work would be completed on the same day it came in.
Question 2: Is any one step a duplicate of another step?	Ask for the reason	Keep the step.	For example, if someone is sorting and another person resorts the same documents, you should ask "why?" before eliminating the duplicate steps.
Question 3: Are there multiple review steps?	Ask for the reason.	N/A	The team will use two tools. First, the Five Why's: the answer to the last why will be the effect/problem in the other tool, the cause and effect diagram. This will lead to developing improvement ideas.
Question 4: Are there loopbacks in this process?	Ask, the reason for the loopbacks. One step should move a document straight to the next step. If not, it is probably stalled or returned to a previous step. We call this a loopback. Loopbacks cause rework and more time in the process	N/A	Conduct a first pass yield calculation to get a sense of the size of the problem. If the calculation proves a small percentage, attribute it to random human error. If more than 30% you need to collect more data. There may be several causes, but you want the most probable cause, so use the cause and effect tool to move you to a solution. When you have the most probable cause collect more data. If the most probable cause is not clear enough to move to a solution, drill down by using the Five Why's Tool.

Figure 3.19   Step-by-step analysis tool

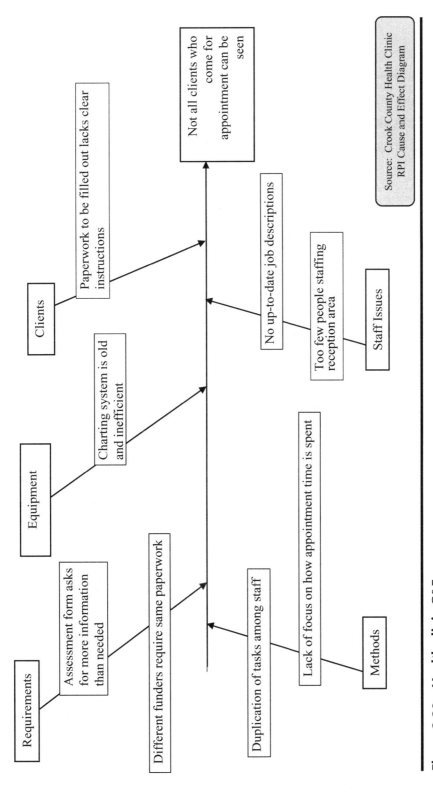

Figure 3.20 Health clinic C&E

Cause and Effect Diagram

There are four steps to using this tool.

1. Identify the problem.

2. Work out the major factors involved.

3. Identify possible causes.

4. Analyze your diagram.

Step 1.

Find a blank piece of paper, large. Draw a rectangle form to the far right of the page. From the left side, draw a solid line across the page to the rectangle.

In the rectangle box, write the problem for which are trying to find the cause(es). (Think of the wording of the problem from the viewpoint of the customer.)

Step 2.

Think of labels or categories of factors that affect that problem. (e.g. People, Materials, Equipment, etc.)

Depending on the number of factors, draw the same amount of diagonal lines spaced evenly on either side of the line across the page that attaches to the problem box.

Step 3.

For each factor, think of specific causes in that category that could cause the problem. Write on a small sticky note...one cause per sticky note. Write as many as you can think of for each category. Then put each sticky note on the flipchart paper where you think it belongs.

Step 4.

Once all the sticky notes are up, step back and look at the entire flipchart paper. (Questions to ask: do the sticky notes congregate around one category the most? If you have more than one person developing the diagram, do you see duplicates being put on the chart? What does that tell you?)

Since there is rarely just one cause, ask yourself or your team, "what are the three most probable causes?" Then go to the flipchart and write on the sticky note you chose, the number 1, 2, or 3.

There are several things you can now do with this information:

You may feel the probable causes need more detail. You can use the 5 Why's tool to drill down to more specifics about the cause. That will refine the cause and lead you to devise more specific actions.

You may want to rank these three causes according to how easy it is to tackle them and come up with an action that addresses the problem.

Figure 3.21   Cause and effect instructions

The 5 Whys is a technique used to analyze a problem; and in many cases can be completed without a data collection plan.

By repeatedly asking the question "Why" (five is a good rule of thumb), you can peel away the layers of symptoms which can lead to the root cause of a problem. Very often the possible (but not sure) reason for a problem will lead you to another question. Although this technique is called "5 Whys," you may find that you will need to ask the question fewer or more times than five before you find the issue related to a problem.

1. Write down the specific problem. Writing the issue helps you formalize the problem and describe it completely. It also helps a team focus on the same problem.

2. Ask Why the problem happens and write the answer down below the problem.

3. If the answer you just provided doesn't identify the root cause of the problem that you wrote down in Step 1, ask Why again and write that answer down.

4. Loop back to step 3 until the team is in agreement that the problem's root cause is identified. Again, this may take fewer or more times than five Whys.

5. The final Why leads the team to a statement (root cause) that the team can take action upon.

Figure 3.22   Five Why's instructions

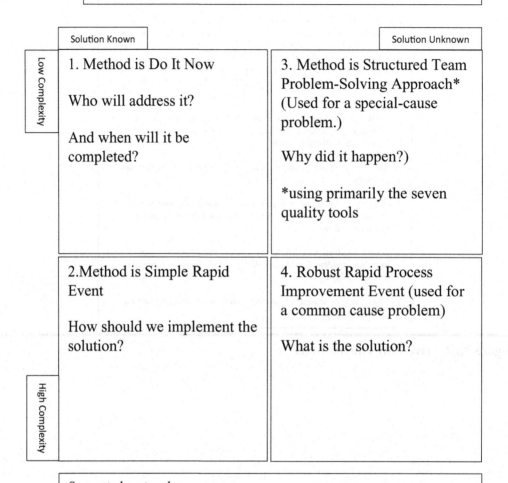

Complexity Solution Matrix

	Solution Known	Solution Unknown
Low Complexity	1. Method is Do It Now Who will address it? And when will it be completed?	3. Method is Structured Team Problem-Solving Approach* (Used for a special-cause problem.) Why did it happen?) *using primarily the seven quality tools
High Complexity	2.Method is Simple Rapid Event How should we implement the solution?	4. Robust Rapid Process Improvement Event (used for a common cause problem) What is the solution?

Suggested protocols:
1. Low Complexity; Solution Known (brainstorming, affinity diagramming, fill our Plan, Do, Check, Act (PDCA) Form, and action plan.
2. Low Complexity; Solution Unknown (develop cause and effect diagram, move from root cause to brainstorming solutions, fill out PDCA form. Test the solution. Action plan.
3. High Complexity, Solution Known (map the process, annotate on map where solution should take place, fill out PDCA forms. Test. Action plan.
4. High Complexity, Solution Unknown (Rapid Process Improvement charter, process mapping, baseline measures, collect and display data, take waste out, make for a continuous flow. PDCA forms. Test and action plan. Final report out.

Figure 3.23 Complexity/Solution Matrix

Chapter 4

Pause
Workshop Quality Check

Why the Pause?

(In the last chapter, we reviewed the options for how long a workshop should be. We reviewed the Complexity/Solution Matrix and the different quadrants. From this point forward, we are addressing the #4 Quadrant, Robust RPI Method option.

At this point, the team has learned much about the current state by walking through the work area and studying all background materials in their packets. When they first started the RPI, they didn't know much about the problem. Now they do. It is probable that the team is starting to question whether they can be successful in the time given. It is also possible that when the charter was developed, the sponsor may have had limited knowledge about the extent of the problem and picking the right goals and measures. It is especially important, that you, the facilitator, address these concerns with the team. You do not want them to stew in their own doubts.)

Review Accomplishments and Learnings

<u>Say in your own words:</u> It is important that we acknowledge what we have accomplished and learned. Here is a list. Please call out what you would add. *(This step will certainly increase the team's morale.)*

(INSTRUCTIONS: Have this list already drawn on the flowchart and at first, covered up.

- learned how their work was structured into processes.
- understood a charter.
- walked through a process, took notes, and interviewed staff.
- analyzed background data including laws and policies.
- developed a new flowchart due to "cleaning up" the old process by taking out unnecessary/waste steps.
- learned basic rudiments of root cause analysis and made simple improvements.
- documented all changes with plan, do, study, act (PDSA) forms.)

Revisit Charter and Change If Necessary

Do Output Measures Relate to the Customer's Needs and Expectations?

Say: I think it is important to revisit our charter.

Say in your own words: Please take the charter out from your background packets. I want you to think about what is being measured in the charter.

Organizations that seek out their customers' needs and expectations know what they must measure to determine if their processes are working. Tools exist to help with this: these include customer surveys and Customer Trees, often called Customer to Quality (CTQ) diagrams.

(INSTRUCTIONS: Read aloud the quote in Figure 4.1.)

> "There have been many RPI's where there are a lot of data and numerous measures. There is the data collected about the process itself, about the number of products, or services. The output measure should be focused on what the customer wants or needs, and that is usually a quality and efficiency measure. It is important here, for you, as the facilitator, to ensure that these measures are tied to the customer."
>
> - S.P. O'Brien, "Lean for the Nonprofit, What You Don't Know Can Cost You"

Figure 4.1 About RPI data

(INSTRUCTIONS: Handout Phone Bank Customer Tree from Appendix 4.)

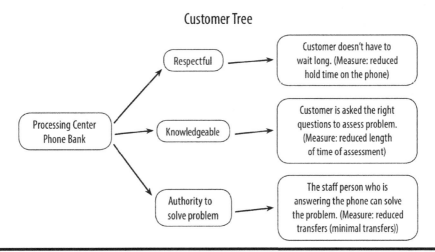

Figure 4.2   Phone bank customer tree

Say in your own words: The handout, a Customer Tree, is a tool that would benefit all managers of processes. The customer tree has three columns. The first column names the Tree. To the right, the second column lists what a customer expects from speaking to a person at the phone center: that they are respectful, knowledgeable, and have the authority to solve the problem. And the third column lists customer's needs and expectations that can be measured. This column can easily identify the outputs of this process. It doesn't have to be complicated. Think about it: when you call a phone bank, the output measure seems like common sense, it is "the number of instances where information is provided."

(INSTRUCTIONS: Have a discussion with the team. Note any comments on a flipchart.

Remind the team that Lean's focus is on the customer and whatever they request, require, or want has to be measured. Ask the team to think about whether the measures on the charter reflect what the customer wants.)

Are the Targets Reasonable for the Team to Reach?

(INSTRUCTIONS: Review the workshop charter and its goals and targets.)
(The team may be wondering whether they can achieve the targets. Hopefully, there is no problem with the current targets and the team can move on with their work. But if there are no targets written at all, or they are

unclear, e.g., "…target is simply better than last year," or the percentages associated with the target goals are disconcerting to the team, this all has to be addressed with the team and sponsor.)

Say in your own words: The target is the percentage of either increase or reduction of measurement that is tied to that goal. Increase or reduction is determined by comparison to a previous measure. Goals are the improvements to be achieved that are expressed in measures of time, or cost, or quality. Goals are set by the sponsor before the workshop starts. The charter has some wording that will describe improvement in terms of time, cost, or quality that affect the output of the process. For example, let's look at the process from the perspective of "time." First, we would carefully word a measure for "time", such as "the time it takes to determine whether a client is eligible for a certain program service or benefit." We would collect data about this measurement before the workshop starts. This is called the baseline data. After improvements are made, we would take the same measurement. And then we would calculate what percentage of that improvement was achieved. That is the target.

(INSTRUCTIONS: Discuss with the team any comments they have about the targets. At this time, it is only the sponsor who can change the targets. If appropriate, invite the sponsor to come to the team room to hear the concerns of the RPI team. Based on this discussion, revise the charter if necessary.)

(If the sponsor meets with the team, it may become clear that the sponsor is not sure how he/she came up with the target. If it was pulled out of thin air, the team has a viable concern. If the targets are too general that is not acceptable. You, as the facilitator, will need to work privately with the sponsor to address the targets and report back to the team. Here are some suggestions: To set a realistic target, you can use historical data from the organization. If there are no historical data, then you can use research from the benchmarks of similar industries or organizations (addressed in Chapter 1.))

Is the Rest of the Charter Clear Enough? Can It Stand Alone?

Say in your own words: Take a minute to read the whole charter. Note any questions you may have. I want to show you an example of another charter and the questions that RPI team had about it.

Team Leader (for Implementation and Evaluation):	Nelda, RN	Facilitator: Paddy
		Name, Office/Unit
Team Members	Nelda, Karen, Kris, Wendy, Mariah, Jessica	
Sponsor(s)	Muriel, RN	
Problems/Need for Workshop: (1-3 bullets):	• Long exams increase costs. • Decreased revenue. • Wait time is so extensive, clients drop-out.	
Primary Goal of Workshop:	To improve customer service. Reduce cost, through increased efficiency.	
Scope:	Clinic flow from time clients seek service to when they leave with prescription or treatment plan.	
Baseline Data:	None at this time.	
Key Dependencies:	Dependent on resources: staff, supplies, computers.	
Expected Benefits (Qualitative):	More people successfully accessing the services. Public image improved. Employee morale increased.	
Targets: Indicators/Metrics (Quantitative):	Increase number of clients seen by 75%. Decrease exam process time by 25%. Decrease clinic visit cycle time by 25%. Increase revenue by 50%.	
Major Deliverables:	Improvements in establishing standards for exam flow and evidence of increased revenue due to influx of clients.	
Timing and Logistics:	Event Date/Time Location WS C. County Health Department Conference Room Planning Aug.1st + Conduct: 9-5, Oct. 27; 8-11:30, Oct. 28 Followup: 30 days post workshop Sustain Improvements: Track one measure: goal of 2.5 clients per hour through the clinic. Complete time studies monthly.	

Figure 4.3   Example: County Health Clinic RPI Charter

(INSTRUCTIONS: Hand out the County RPI Charter from Appendix 4.)

Say: Please read this charter in the handout and tell me the comments you have; I will record them on the flipchart. *(Give the team time to absorb the list on the flipchart.)*

Say in your own words: The County Health Clinic RPI team had a lot of questions about their charter.

(INSTRUCTIONS: (Handout: RPI team questions about the charter from Appendix 4.) Read aloud the County RPI team questions about the charter. As you are reading aloud, pause to let the team absorb. Take questions during these pauses.)

Preparing for the Next Level of Improvements: The New Pathway Model

<u>Say in your own words:</u> Our new Pathway Model has two phases of improvement work. We have accomplished our first phase of improvements of removing the unnecessary steps, i.e., cleaning up our process.

The second phase of improvements focuses not on specific steps, but on the **flow** of the work. We want to make our process flow smoothly. Remember when we did our walk-through, we collected the amount of time that lapsed in between process steps. This highlighted delays in the process. We also analyzed loopbacks in the process. Loopbacks denoted a possible need to make corrections to work already done. This was rework. Delays and rework add costs, and do not enable a smooth flow.

(INSTRUCTIONS: Hand out What impedes flow? from Appendix 4.)

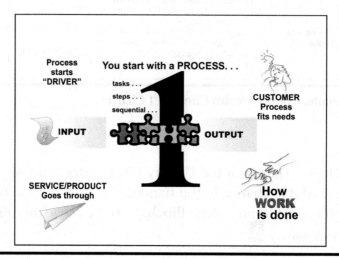

Figure 4.4   Components of a process: What can impede flow

This handout shows how all components of a process can impede a smooth flow. The input from the supplier, the process steps in the middle, and the output that is delivered to the customer. Take a look.

Discuss. *(This is another instance of leading them back to process thinking.)*

The Model

(INSTRUCTIONS: Draw Figure 4.5 on the flipchart.)

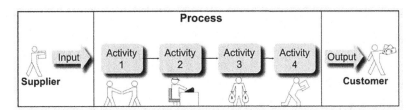

Figure 4.5   Three-part schematic process

<u>Say in your own words:</u> The model we are going to use in the second phase of improvements replicates the components of a process. We are going to smooth out the process by dividing up the improvement work into these parts, the input, the process steps, and the output. *(It has been my experience that dividing the work like this, makes it much more manageable for the team. I got this idea from the number of RPI teams I facilitated who were in the midst of developing their improvement recommendations and they had to stop and ask, "And* <u>where</u> *will this improvement be made?" You will find that this model will streamline the work of the team.)*

(INSTRUCTIONS: Circle the input part of the flipchart.)

<u>Say:</u> This is where the work comes into the process.

(INSTRUCTIONS: Circle process/activities part on the flipchart.)

<u>Say in your own words:</u> Two kinds of improvements go into this process/activities part: improvements concerning "how the work goes through the process" and improvements concerning "how the work is performed." The performance of the work directly impacts the output. (INSTRUCTIONS: Circle the output part of the flipchart.)

<u>Say in your own words:</u> Something is included in this model that we don't normally see: the **supports** of the process such as human resources,

information systems, and/or services. These are an integral part of all improvement recommendations.

(Always monitor the energy of the team during the workshop. Note when they need some activity. Keep a stash of appropriate exercises/case studies to pull out to use when you need to energize the team. One such activity is the next exercise.)

Say in your own words: To get us ready for the next level of improvements regarding flow, we are going to do an exercise.

FACILITATOR INSTRUCTIONS FOR NEWSLETTER EXERCISE

SUPPLIES FOR NEWSLETTER EXERCISE

1. (15) blank pieces of 8x10 paper,
2. (15) legal-sized envelopes,
3. small round stickers (30),
4. stamp and pad,
5. small address labels (20),
6. a bowl with an 1/2 inch of water and a small 1-inch cube sponge,
7. a letter tray,
8. a letter opener,
9. and a cleared table with 5 chairs around it equidistant from each other.

Explain the roles for the exercise: Timer will note time from the beginning to the end of the entire process. Folder will fold the piece of paper in thirds. Stuffer will put paper in envelope and use the sponge to seal the envelope. Address Labeler will put the address label in the middle of the front of the envelope. Postage person will put a "postage stamp" (red dot) in the right-hand corner and the "return address" label in the left corner.

Figure 4.6   Newsletter instructions partial

(INSTRUCTIONS: Retrieve one copy of the handout for yourself. Facilitator Instructions for the Newsletter Exercise in Appendix 4. Closely follow them.)

Say: This exercise is called the Newsletter Exercise. I need five volunteers to take on a role while the rest of you observe and take notes. The volunteers will sit at the table. *(Make sure you have cleared a table and have put (15) blank pieces of 8 × 10 paper, (15) legal-sized envelopes, small round stickers (30), stamp and pad, small address labels (20), a bowl with 1/2 inch of water and a small one-inch cube sponge, a letter opener, and a letter tray. Complete the exercise.)*

Say in your own words: The purpose of this exercise was to familiarize you with what and where a smooth process can be impeded.

You may, at this point, wonder about all the work we have already done. It will be brought forward to use in this part of the workshop. For example, when we get to Chapter 6, "Smooth Out the Flow: The Work Going Through the Process", we will look at the wait times between the steps collected in Chapter 1. Our aim is to shrink those wait times to smooth out the flow. We will also use measurements of time that we collected in the step-by-step analysis in Chapter 3, "Improve: Clean Up the Current Process". When we get to Chapter 7, "Smooth Out the Flow: Improve How the Work Is Performed", we will bring forward the loopbacks that we noted in the step-by-step exercise and use our learnings of root cause analysis (from Chapter 3). And when we get to Chapter 8, "Smooth Out the Flow: Improve Process Supports", we will use the handoff charts, the spaghetti charts, and the blueprint/floorplan we completed in Chapter 2, "Understanding the Current State".

List of Facilitation Deliverables

- Completed PDSA forms.
- Revised charter (signed off by Sponsor)

The Art of Facilitation: Balance Three Things at Once

The PowerPoint slide below depicts what happens with your head and your heart as you facilitate. While you are doing "that facilitator thing" with three balls in the air at once (1. turning a group of separate individuals into a team quickly, 2. making sure the team is "taught in the moment" when necessary, and 3. managing the team's progress), you are also becoming aware of "all that enters" the team room on the first day…all the things that you have no control over! (Figure 4.14 Presentation to Lean Leaders. – S.P. O'Brien.)

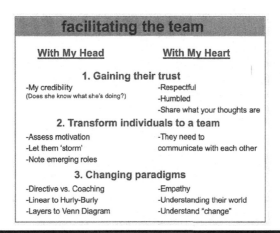

Figure 4.7   Presentation to Lean Leaders, Dept. of Human Services

Appendix 4

HANDOUTS:

HANDOUTS just for facilitator:

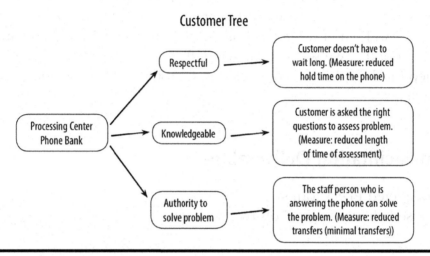

Figure 4.8   Phone bank customer tree

Team Leader (for Implementation and Evaluation):	Nelda, RN	Facilitator: Paddy
		Name, Office/Unit
Team Members	Nelda, Karen, Kris, Wendy, Mariah, Jessica	
Sponsor(s)	Muriel, RN	
Problems/Need for Workshop: (1-3 bullets):	• Long exams increase costs. • Decreased revenue. • Wait time is so extensive, clients drop-out.	
Primary Goal of Workshop:	To improve customer service. Reduce cost, through increased efficiency.	
Scope:	Clinic flow from time clients seek service to when they leave with prescription or treatment plan.	
Baseline Data:	None at this time.	
Key Dependencies:	Dependent on resources: staff, supplies, computers.	
Expected Benefits (Qualitative):	More people successfully accessing the services. Public image improved. Employee morale increased.	
Targets: Indicators/Metrics (Quantitative):	Increase number of clients seen by 75%. Decrease exam process time by 25%. Decrease clinic visit cycle time by 25%. Increase revenue by 50%.	
Major Deliverables:	Improvements in establishing standards for exam flow and evidence of increased revenue due to influx of clients.	
Timing and Logistics:	**Event Date/Time Location** WS C. County Health Department Conference Room Planning Aug.1st + Conduct: 9-5, Oct. 27; 8-11:30, Oct. 28 Followup: 30 days post workshop Sustain Improvements: Track one measure: goal of 2.5 clients per hour through the clinic. Complete time studies monthly.	

Figure 4.9   County Health Clinic Patient Processes RPI

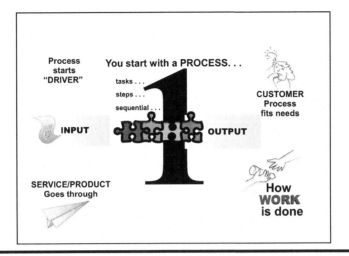

Figure 4.10   What impedes flow

There were several comments and questions the team had about this charter (besides "no baseline data" provided on the charter).

1. Scope: "Clinic flow from time clients seek service to when they leave with a prescription or treatment plan." Team comments: "This is not exactly clear. In the scope, what constitutes the <u>start</u> of 'seeking service'? Can it be just a phone call or is it a clinic visit?"

2. Targets: How were these targets set? What data did the sponsor have to set a target? If the sponsor just pulled the target out of thin air, this needs to be revisited. Researching benchmarks from other like organizations would be helpful.

3. Targets: The team had read background about the clinic. They knew that the clinic used a sliding scale to charge fees. Team asked: "If this is a government county clinic, and they determine fees on a sliding scale, how can they think they could 'increase revenue by 50%?"

4. Problems/Need for Workshop: Long exams increase costs. Decrease revenue. Wait time is so extensive, that clients drop out. Team comments: "It appears that data needs to be collected about the issue of revenue. Also, how do they know clients drop out? Do they have data on people who come in and then leave. This is a very different piece of data than a 'no-show.' Do they have data on the number of teens and WIN clients that are seen?"

Figure 4.11   County Health Clinic RPI Team questions about the flowchart

FACILITATOR INSTRUCTIONS FOR NEWSLETTER EXERCISE

SUPPLIES FOR NEWSLETTER EXERCISE

1. (15) blank pieces of 8x10 paper,
2. (15) legal-sized envelopes,
3. small round stickers (30),
4. stamp and pad,
5. small address labels (20),
6. a bowl with an 1/2 inch of water and a small 1-inch cube sponge,
7. a letter tray,
8. a letter opener,
9. and a cleared table with 5 chairs around it equidistant from each other.

Explain the roles for the exercise: <u>Timer</u> will note time from the beginning to the end of the entire process. <u>Folder</u> will fold the piece of paper in thirds. <u>Stuffer</u> will put paper in envelope and use the sponge to seal the envelope. <u>Address Labeler</u> will put the address label in the middle of the front of the envelope. <u>Postage person</u> will put a "postage stamp" (red dot) in the right-hand corner and the "return address" label in the left corner.

<u>Demonstrate how to do it.</u> Have the team work with one piece of paper and walk them through each step. Hover. Make sure they get it right.

<u>Explain how the exercise moves along.</u> The team will do two rounds of ten documents each. Tell the team the rules: 1. no talking and 2. each person at their own station must finish all 10 pieces of paper before they can pass them on to the next person. The rest of the RPI Team will observe and take notes of what they see in Round 1.

The timer will start when the work begins with the first person and will end when the last step is done on the last item. The Timer will record the cycle time of the first round on a flipchart piece of paper.

Round 2: Explain that the rules are going to change for this round. Explain that they will be given 10 of everything this time, the same as last time. But now, each person, once they finish their task on one item, will pass it on to the next person right away. Then they begin working on the second item, and so on. The timer will start when the work begins with the first person and will end when the last step is done on the last item. The timer will record the time on the same flip chart piece of paper.

<u>Facilitator lead discussion about learnings from this exercise.</u> The team will look at the two different rounds and see how much less time it took in the second round. Ask the team, what additional changes would they make to the process if there was a Round 3? (Point out other improvements that could be made like combining tasks and adding one more staff to an overburdened position or rearranging the seating.)

Figure 4.12   Instructions for the newsletter exercise

SELF-STUDY: Example of a complete and accurate charter, Payroll Timekeeping RPI

Team Leader	Becky D.		Facilitator	Paddy O'Brien
	Name			**Unit**
Team Members	Bonnie R.			Proc. Ctr., Mgr.
	Ellen R.			OHP Proc. Ctr.
	Michelle B.			Payroll
	Robin D.			CAF Field
	Laer H.			OIS
	Sharon M.			Payroll
	Cam F.			Human Resources
	Debbie G.			OSH-Food Services
Sponsor	Shawn J.			
Problem Definition	Nothing adversely affects employee morale more than problems with their pay. "Locking time" is a function performed by managers who are responsible to review, validate, and approve "time worked" that is inputted into the system by the employees the manager is responsible for. Employees are responsible for checking their available leave hours before they request it. Over ¼ of all Department of Human Services (DHS) employees (2500) have not had their time locked by their managers every month. As a result, employees are not paid on time and staff expends time in corrections and expediting special payments. In addition, there are grievances filed by employees that must be resolved and there are Bureau of Labor and Industries violations that must also be resolved.			
Scope	The scope will involve the analysis and subsequent streamlining to the "locking time" process. This will begin with Payroll verifying if the OSPS Leave Accrual Reports are used and submitted to supervisory managers and end when the employee is paid correctly. (Sub-processes: Requesting and Inputting Time, Ensuring Employees are Paid, Processing Timesheets, Correcting Timesheets.)			
Objectives	To improve and standardize a process for time locking that ensures that all DHS employees are paid accurately and timely. To develop future state reports that will meet customer needs.			
Timeframe	Planning: June 18-July 27 Conduct: August 20, 21, 22 Follow up: August 23, Sept.1			
Baseline Data	• 10,752 corrections a year.			

(a)

Figure 4.13 Payroll Timekeeping RPI Charter

	• 3336 special checks a year.
	• 120,000 paper timesheets a year.
	• 720 overpayments a year.
	• 20% error rate in process.
	• Process steps: 53 steps; Handoffs: 14.
Major Deliverable	• Improvements to current policies and procedures.
	• Improved locking time process (that addresses the people, methods, materials, equipment and environment components of the process.
	• Reduction of employee timesheet corrections.
	• Cost savings due to payroll employees' time spent on processing, expediting, correcting and disseminating incorrect payments.
	• Accountability and responsibility and timelines added to current policy and procedures.
	• Cost savings related to attorney fees with DOJ.
Key Performance Indicators	• Incorrect payments (#'s of, and dollar amounts).
	• Grievances and complaints.
	• Cycle time (labor hours to do data pulls and prepare report).
	• Cost of processing corrections.
Targets	Reduction of time sheet corrections by 50% within 60 days and 100% in 6 months.
	Reduction of issue of special checks by 50% in 60 days.
	Eliminate paper timesheet distribution and processing.
	Eliminate the need to process overpayments.
	Increase the collection or resolution of current overpayments:

(b)

Figure 4.13 Payroll Timekeeping RPI Charter. (Continued).

Chapter 5

Smooth Out the Flow:

Improve the Process When the Work Comes In

Prep Work: Understand the Current State of "Input"

<u>Say in your own words:</u> When the work coming into the process (the input) is not managed, what happens? If you are behind, you will get more behind. If you are not meeting daily schedules, you may cut corners. If staff are spending the same amount of effort and time on a simple document as a complex one, valuable time and resources are squandered. One of the ways we manage our work is to prioritize or sort the work right at the beginning.

(Following are work activities for the team to complete in this chapter. These activities involve collecting and verifying information on the "input.")

(INSTRUCTIONS: Draw on a flipchart:

- Data
- Kinds of products/services
- Controlling/distributing work
- Points of entry)

Say in your own words: (pointing to the flipchart)
This list represents all the things to consider with the input part of a process.
(INSTRUCTIONS: Read aloud the following as you go through the list.

Data: Are there data collected about what is coming into the organization to be worked on?
Kinds of products/services: Are there different types of documents coming in, e.g., applications, reapplications, and renewals?
Controlling/and distributing work: When the work comes in, how does the staff access it?
Points of entry: Are all points of entry of the incoming work identified?)

Ask for volunteers to self-assign to work on the items on the flipchart and have them write their name by the item.

Data Collection. Background/Information

Say in your own words: Many organizations do not even know how much work is coming in. But there are examples of organizations which do. Let me show you.
(INSTRUCTIONS: Draw on the flipchart, the information in Figure 5.1.)
The data on the flipchart represents what comes into the organization as work products: phone calls to make and receive, Interactive Voice Response (IVR) calls to respond to, and applications to be processed. Although the RPI was conducted in the first quarter, data for the next three quarters were collected as the improvements were implemented. Comparison of the first quarter to the last quarter showed the progress of the improvements. For example, the number of phone calls decreased due to applications being processed more quickly.
Say in your own words: Here is another example of using incoming data from the Emergency Medical Services RPI: the team collected data that resulted in improvement. By looking at data from the past 2 years, quarter by

	1st Qtr 2004
• Phone Calls	60,391
• IVR Calls	54,236
• Applications Received	54,386
• Applications Processed	57,021
• Hearings Requested	191
• Processing Days Out	42
• Full Time Employees	213
• Overtime Hours	869

Figure 5.1 Example: OHP Processing Center RPI Application Process (incoming work)

quarter, they were able to project how much work would be coming in at certain times and they could staff up accordingly. The data told them December through February was the busiest time for processing Recertification applications. They could expect the following volume of work:

(INSTRUCTIONS: Read aloud:

- Certification Applications numbering between 500 and 1000.
- Phone calls numbering between 50 and 100 a day.
- Emails numbering between 50 and 100 a day.)

Say in your own words: From this information, the manager could figure out how long it takes to process one application or how long the average phone call is, or how long it takes to respond to emails in a day. With that data, the manager could do a simple calculation to see how many hours would be needed to do the work. (Use the Self-Study in Appendix 2, backlog plan, as a point of reference.)

(INSTRUCTIONS: Hand out Payroll Timekeeping RPI Process Timeline from Appendix 5.)

Say in your own words: This is a good example of not only collecting what is coming in, but when. The RPI team discovered that the work staff knew there was fluctuation in the volume of work, but didn't know much more. They just did the work that came to them the best they could. *(One*

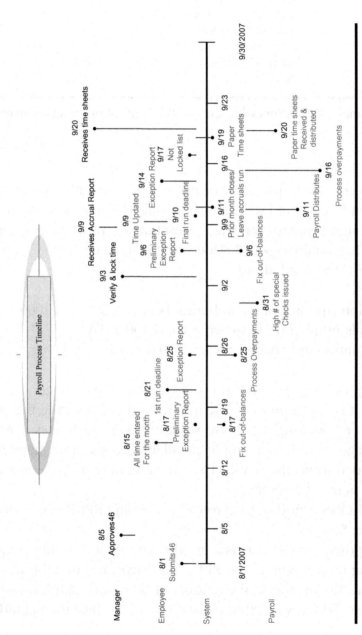

Figure 5.2 Payroll Timekeeping time line. Example: Payroll RPI

time, when I asked a regional manager in the Human Services field office how he prioritized his work, he told me, "I don't pay much attention to what comes in, I just look at the top of my inbox every morning and start from there!")

Some workers, in one part of the Payroll process, knew their deadlines, and others, in another part of the process knew theirs. But no one had the big picture. No one in the entire process knew the regular dates <u>when</u> certain documents came in. The RPI team interviewed the work staff and created the timeline in this handout. This was helpful to the staff so they could anticipate and plan for their work. This was helpful to the manager in adjusting staffing needs.

(INSTRUCTIONS: Assign the volunteers for Data to begin collecting data about the incoming work to the organization. Remind them that if they discover there are no data, they will have to work with the sponsor to create the data or use alternative information. Advise them to refer back to Chapter 1, Handout, "Data Collection Approaches" to refresh their learning. Converse with them about how to get started.)

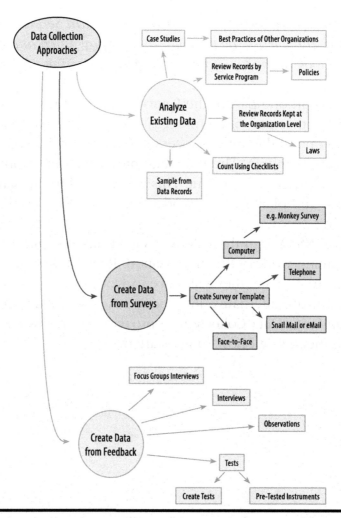

Figure 5.3 Three paths to collecting data: analyze existing data, create data from surveys, or create data from feedback

Kinds of Products/Services. Background/Information

(INSTRUCTIONS: Begin going through the following background information on kinds of products/services. At the end, assign the products/services team to start collecting their information.)

Say in your own words: Many times we don't include ALL products and services that come out of the process. Here are some examples: At the Oregon Nursing Board RPI, we learned that there were different kinds of applications for accreditation that were submitted to the nursing board. This variety created a problem for the RPI team. The RPI team had one flowchart that they were using. The flowchart hadn't taken into consideration all the other kinds of applications. Were there different processes for different applications? The RPI team had to answer the question before they could move on.

(INSTRUCTIONS: Hand out Oregon Board of Nursing Product Family Chart from Appendix 5.)

They filled out a useful tool called a Product Family Chart. This chart was structured like a matrix, so that all the steps for all the different applications were listed across the top of the page while each kind of application was listed down the left side of the page. They were cross-walked and marked with an "x".

(INSTRUCTIONS: Draw an outline of a chart on a whiteboard or flipchart paper. Put an arrow down from top to bottom on the left side of the matrix and mark it "kinds" and put an arrow from the left to the right at the top of the matrix and mark it "steps".)

Nurse Licensing and Certifications Process

	Written application Needed/review	Submitted references review	Criminal Records Check	Required courses reviewed	Internship checked	Reapplication reviewed	Annual exam reviewed
RN	X	X	X	X	X	X	X
BSN	X	X	X		X	X	
CCRN		X	X	X		X	X
MSN		X	X	X		X	X
LPN	X	X	X	X	X		
CNS	X		X		X	X	X
MHR	X		X		X	X	X

Figure 5.4   Example: Product Family Chart, Nursing Board Accreditation RPI

What they learned, depending on the type of application, was that the process steps could vary. For example, an RN (Registered Nurse) application had to go through all seven steps of the process, whereas the CNS (Clinical Nurse Specialist) application only had five steps. (The CNS, the BSN (Bachelor of Science in Nursing), and the MHR (Master of Human Relations) applications don't have the process step for course requirements.)

The RPI team wondered if they needed to develop many flowcharts depending on the type of application. The truth is they didn't have time. What was the alternative? They chose to use the Product Family Chart to identify the one application process that covered all the steps in all the application processes.

They chose the RN certification process to amend their initial flowchart.

The Product Family Chart also showed them the steps that appeared for every kind of application. When the team got to examining the workflow, they looked closely at the "criminal records check" step and the "reapplication reviewed" step. Improvements in these areas had a far-reaching effect.

(INSTRUCTIONS: Send the volunteers working on Kinds of Products/Services to collect information. Their goal is to ensure that they have knowledge about all the different types of products and services that come out of the process (es). Coach them where to start.)

Controlling/Distributing Work. Background/Information

Say in your own words: So far, we have collected incoming data and gained knowledge of different types of products/services requested by a customer. But there is another challenge: most staff are overwhelmed and pressured with the work that comes in and they scramble every day to get it done.

Here are examples of managing the work as it comes in. Please listen as I read a couple of examples that include the problem and the solution.

(INSTRUCTIONS: You can pick one or two of the following examples to read aloud.)

Example 1: from the Metro Food Stamp Processing Center RPI. The snail mail comes in, is date-stamped, screened to determine the type of document it is, and filed into one of several bucket bins that holds work to be done.

Staff go from their workstation to one of the buckets, and choose their work for the day. They can choose what kind of documents to work on and how many. The bucket bins are labelled as either (1) Redeterminations, (2) Changes and Miscellaneous, and (3) 859's. This way of choosing work for the day created an unevenness in the workload.

Solution: Instead of having the workers go pick a stack of applications to work on for the day, the Lead Worker prepared packets of applications to be worked on for each worker each day. At the end of the day, he retrieved what remained in the worker's packet to build a new packet for the next day. The Lead Worker was able to note what was left in each packet and who might need assistance or training.

Example 2: This is from the Adoptions Coos County RPI. One of the incoming pieces of work was the huge volume of phone calls that had to be answered. This was bothersome to the adoption workers in Coos County. They were lamenting that they never seem to get anything done.

One of the adoption workers said, "I'm busy, that's for sure, but what a mess! I don't know what I accomplish."

The facilitator asked the adoption workers to track their time for 3 weeks daily in 15-minute intervals. This is what the time-tracking data revealed about all these incoming calls: Incoming calls on a daily basis came into a central receptionist who transferred 95% of the calls to the adoption workers. (She tracked the number of calls she responded to and the number that she transferred to others to handle.)

The workers were constantly being interrupted by these transfers because there was no escape. Transfers went straight to the worker's desk and if they didn't pick up, a loudspeaker announced their name and they had to take the call.

Solution: The RPI Team recommended setting up "protected time" for the Adoptions Unit so that no phone or pager or loudspeaker interruptions happen during this time. The RPI set up a pilot test: During protected time, phone calls will go to voice mail and adoption workers will not be paged during protected time. The supervisor will handle all "emergencies" and will only interrupt a worker when deemed absolutely necessary. The entire staff will be notified of the pilot test. There will be special coordination with reception staff and others who might be at the front desk. This pilot test will take place over a 5-week period.

Say in your own words: In another situation, we have to ask, what happens when work is segregated into simple and complex?

Not all work that comes into the organization is the same in regards to complexity. Yet many offices give just as much attention, time, and effort to the simple as well as the complex. Grocery stores realized the inefficiencies of not sorting work up front a long time ago a long time ago and instituted express lanes.

Example 3: from the OHP Ombudsman Call Process RPI. The number of problems coming in the phone calls to the Ombudsman was overwhelming.

Figure 5.5 Grocery Store Express Lane

Anyone in the office could pick up the phone but not everyone had the skills to solve the problem.

<u>Solution:</u> The solution was to set up a screening system that could rank the kind of problem that was being phoned about. Whoever answered the phone could ask a few standard questions, and depending on the answers, the worker could solve the problem or pass the call on to the appropriate person.

Example 4: from the Field Offices Client Application Process RPI. At one of the field offices where people come in to get different kinds of help such as asking a question, submitting an application, or showing up for an appointment, the process was fraught with long waits for <u>everyone</u>. This brought on a lot of complaints, especially from clients who wanted to just drop something off and didn't need to talk or meet with anyone.

<u>Solution:</u> The RPI team collected more data about the kinds of services people needed when they came to the office. The team was able to develop new signage in the reception area and have three different reception stations appropriate to the clients' business. (And yes, they included a mail slot for 'drop-offs'.)

Example 5: from the Human Resources Personnel Action Process RPI. The team found out that the required personnel form could be submitted in more than one format. For instance, someone could drop a filled-out form at the front desk, and at the same time, fax the same form or even attach it to an email. That is three versions of the same form coming into the process. This created duplicate work, resulting in inaccurate recordkeeping.

<u>Solution:</u> A new workflow and work standards were developed and included in a new policy and procedure that was disseminated to the entire organization. This would eliminate duplicative submissions of the same application.

Example 6: from the North Valley Processing Center Applications Process RPI. The team examined the applications that were being kept in an in-box (not laid down in a pile but standing up one after another) just waiting to be worked on. The applications were placed in the in-box according to the date that they came in. The RPI team observed that the workers would go to the box and pick the applications to work on that day. They always chose applications that were in the front of the in-box. That meant that the older applications just kept moving further and further back. This, of course, brought numerous complaints from applicants who had to wait and be without benefits.

<u>Solution:</u> An immediate improvement was to use the FIFO (first in, first out) method where the oldest applications were placed so they would be worked on first.

(INSTRUCTIONS: Send the mini-team, Controlling/Distributing the Work to collect information about how the work gets to the worker. Coach them where to start.)

Points of Entry. Background/Information

<u>Say in your own words:</u> Like having knowledge of different products or services that come out of a process, it is also important to know all the points of entry into a process. If a point of entry is missed, the flowchart is not accurate.

(Read aloud.) This is an example from the Financial Services Receipting Process RPI. The Receipting Unit is the last stop in the process. They are located in a building on the state hospital grounds. They are ultimately responsible for recording all receipts into the organization's financial system. The main problem is that there are many offices throughout the organization who receive receipts. They are located in different buildings. And these different locations may not "talk" to each other.

This creates a secondary problem: there is a lack of proper internal controls over the custody of the receipts. Since so many hands touch this process, things fall through the cracks.

Receipts that come to the Parkway Building go through the Imaging Unit first. They are not logged in. Their only "log" record is an image which is in the imaging system. The Receipting Unit cannot access the imaging system. They get the checks after they are imaged...there is no real proof whether the checks that come to the Parkway Building as the first entry eventually get to the Receipting Unit which is located in another building. This situation created a lack of internal controls and potential for fraud.

The Accounts Receivable (A/R) Unit sets up accounts receivable and sends out invoices. The invoices are notated with a number to correspond to a contract or program. The payments come back to a specific P.O. Box set up for accounts receivable that is located in the basement of the building. The A/R staff retrieves the mail, sorts it, and opens it. Checks and other payments are forwarded to the Receipting Unit. More often than not, the payment enters the receipting process without proper notation of the contract or program number. Trying to match the contract number to the payment creates a lot of rework for the Receipting Unit.

Solution: Like previous examples a new workflow and standard work was included in a new policy and procedure to centralize the receipts of checks and other types of payments. The solution included new training in accounting internal controls for all employees.

(INSTRUCTIONS: Send the mini-team, Points of Entry, out to collect data. Coach them how to start.)

List of Facilitation Deliverables

- Completed PDSA forms.
- List of type and volume of work coming in.

The Art of Facilitation: Work with Your Data

Data, in all its glory may be daunting to the team. Assure them that all the data collection paths on the Data Collection Approaches chart (handed out in Chapter 1) are within the range of their capabilities.

It is important to teach the team about the range of kinds of data collection. In the field of internal auditing, data are collected to support audit findings. "Least reliable data" are those which are more qualitative, anecdotal, or simple observation. "Most reliable" are original documents, feedback from the source, and/or review of existing data reports or sampling.

At the same time, you have to be a judge of how much data is "enough data." A "good rule of thumb" is what Dr. W.E. Deming (engineer who taught statistical analysis to the Japanese after WW II) said: "Collect enough data so you know the pattern."

As the facilitator, you have a critical responsibility regarding data in the workshop: you will have to make sure that the team has done enough work in collecting data before they move on to other work.

Appendix 5

HANDOUTS:

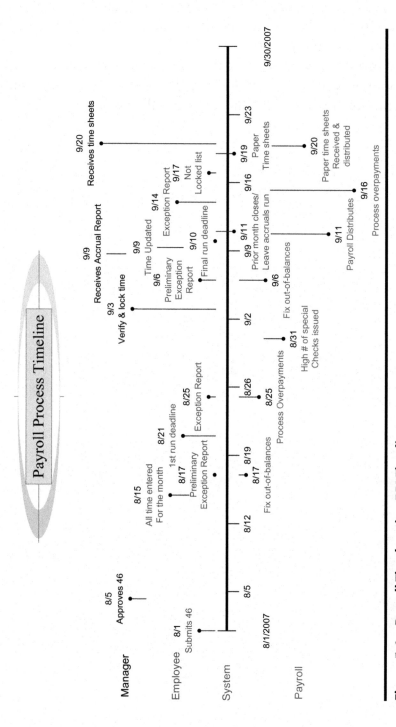

Figure 5.6 Payroll Timekeeping RPI Timeline

Nurse Licensing and Certifications Process

	Written application Needed/review	Submitted references review	Criminal Records Check	Required courses reviewed	Internship checked	Reapplication reviewed	Annual exam reviewed
RN	X	X	X	X	X	X	X
BSN	X	X	X		X	X	
CCRN		X	X	X		X	X
MSN		X	X	X		X	X
LPN	X	X	X	X	X		
CNS	X		X		X	X	X
MHR	X		X		X	X	X

Figure 5.7   Oregon Board of Nursing Accreditation Process RPI Product Family Chart

Chapter 6

Smooth Out the Flow:

Improve the Work as It Goes Through the Process

Minimize Batching

<u>Say in your own words:</u> I am going to talk about concepts and tools to improve a process as the work is going through it. The first concept is batching. At the end of this overview, I am going to ask for volunteers to look at batching in the process we are trying to improve.

Remember your economics class and the term "economies of scale"? People have been used to thinking in terms of economies of scale (i.e., moving more goods and services on a larger scale)…so they think moving big batches of materials and info is better than smaller batches or one piece flow. In Lean, any gains achieved through economies of scale are offset by the waste of having to move and store big batches of documents or materials.

This may have made sense at one time in large organizations where there was mass production. But in a Lean organization, there is no mass production so the work has to flow differently. Remember the newsletter exercise we did in the last chapter (Chapter 5)? We had to store a large supply of paper and other materials to get that newsletter collated and then disseminated. We learned many things about a process and how to improve it. When we stopped batching our work (i.e., holding on to it until the task was completed on all 10 newsletters at one work station before it was passed on to another work station) and replaced it with one-piece flow, it was faster. One advantage of one-piece flow is that it can allow us to stop the current processes mid-stream. This is necessary when customers unexpectedly change their requirements mid-processing and the process flow may have to be tweaked.

Say in your own words: Let me give you examples…

(INSTRUCTIONS: Pick one of the examples to read aloud.)

Example 1: regarding batching from the Archives RPI. The Archives staff noted, that at the end of the month they have an influx of boxes of records coming to the warehouse in Salem to be stored. This is because the Portland metro area offices (40 miles away) send all their storage boxes in batches in one huge delivery at the end of each month. Every month, there is money spent on overtime for the Archives staff to catch up on the work. If the deliveries were made periodically throughout the month, the staff would be able to implement continuous flow.

(Read aloud.) Example 2: regarding batching from the Hospital Patients Transitioning to Community Services RPI. The focus process was transitioning patients from Oregon State Hospital to community care facilities. The facilities had to have a new or amended contract with Mental Health Services. It's important to pay these facilities so they continue to provide services. The process starts with a filled-out Pink Form that initiates encumbrances to the program services budget and starts the writing of a contract or contract amendment to pay for those services. Two different staff groups work on this process; the Community Care Staff and the Contracts Staff. The RPI team discovered that the Community Care Staff batched all these pink forms and turned them over to the Contract Staff monthly. This overwhelmed the Contracts staff. They spent much of the weekend working to catch up on processing the Pink Forms. The Contracts manager requested that batching cease and that daily deliveries of the forms be delivered to the contracts office.

Say in your own words: I need two volunteers to collect information and data about batching practices in the current process and bring back the information to the team.

(INSTRUCTIONS: Give them instructions for researching the amount of batching going on in the process:

1. Find out where batching is taking place in the process.
2. Determine what the batch sizes are.
3. Interview workers and collect data to see if reduced batch sizes or no batching is feasible.
4. Return to the team room and fill out a PDSA form for a pilot test and report out to the rest of the team.)

Introduce Error-Proofing

<u>Say in your own words:</u> Here is another concept that can improve the work flow of a process: error-proofing.

Mistakes always happen. But if you can catch them early, and correct them right away, this saves a lot of resources. Some call this a type of error-proofing. A small mistake or error, made at the beginning of the process, if not detected, gets bigger and more costly as it goes through the process. These errors cause disruption, delay, and money. Setting up error-proofing can save an organization millions of dollars. Here is an example:

<u>Say in your own words:</u> This is from the Metro Food Stamp Processing Center RPI. The Federal government funnels money through state governments to provide food stamps to citizens who apply for benefits. State workers decide whether applicants are eligible for this benefit. After the client has been served, the caseworker documents their decisions in case notes that are filed away. The case is closed and the files are stored.

Six months later, when federal auditors come to the state agency office to see whether or not caseworkers made the right decisions (and therefore used the federal monies prudently), the auditors usually found many mistakes. This resulted in issuing fines to the state agency for huge amounts. If employees were able to stop what they were doing, and correct their own mistakes ("right at the source") (a Lean premise), significant money would be saved.

If staff do not work in a Lean environment, many organizations frown on workers stopping their work to correct their own mistake or ask for help. These workers continue to fear making mistakes and then continue to make them.

(The Lean factory has an Andon cord which usually hangs near where the work is being done. When a worker needs help, they pull the cord. This stops the line, and people gather in a small huddle to solve the problem.

Also, note that many Lean managers know about Dr. W. Edwards Deming, quality leader. He created 14 Points (or rules) for management. Rule #8 applies here: "Reduce fear throughout the organization by encouraging open, two-way communication. Drive out fear." There is freedom in the factory to pull the Andon cord and ask for help.)

In Chapter 3, we conducted the step-by-step analysis and noted loopbacks in the process flow. Loopbacks usually indicate mistakes have been made when a task is performed and documents have to be sent back to be corrected. This is called "rework" and costs time and resources. Also, in Chapter 3, we learned how to determine whether errors are a one-time occurrence or whether they occur more often, which could indicate a systemic problem. We determined this by interviewing staff and asking how often these loopbacks occurred. Then, based on the answers, we gathered more data for substantiation. Then, with the information, we calculated the Completion/Accuracy percentage. We knew that if the resulting percentage is above a certain number, then we can safely say this is systemic error, not a one-time human error.

Ask: Can you give me some examples of error-proofing from work or everyday life? (To get them started, you can mention: "highlighting input areas on forms, implementing controls over electronic data input to restrict a field, and designing cable connectors so that they can only be inserted in one way.")

Say in your own words: I need two volunteers to collect information and data about applying error-proofing in the current process and bring back that information to the team.

(INSTRUCTIONS: Hand out, "Error-proof a process instructions" from Appendix 6 and meet with the volunteers for error-proofing.)

As the facilitator, thoroughly go through the handout with them. Answer any of their questions.

Ask them to come back to the team room, write up a PDSA form, and report back to the rest of the team.

Push or Pull and Kanban

Say in your own words: Here are some more concepts to introduce improvement to the process. They are "push or pull" and "Kanban."

Think about this: when you have work pushed on you and you are already working as hard as you can, you work even harder to keep up. This has consequences. You can get more stressed and probably more behind. But, if you had the option of waiting until you were ready for the next piece of work, and were able to "pull" it towards you, you'd probably be less stressed and your productivity would grow. This is what is meant by "the push or pull method."

Say in your own words: Here are some examples of pull systems in a process:

■ After applications are scanned, the scanning staff puts the applications in a staging area. When the eligibility worker is ready for more work, they pull the applications from the staging area.

■ A familiar everyday example is boarding an airplane. Airline staff at the gate do not call passengers to board until they receive a report that the plane has been cleaned.

(INSTRUCTIONS: Always have the latest flowchart displayed on the wall. The wait times between steps should be marked on the flowchart. Ask for a volunteer from the team to analyze the current flow for push or pull methods. Instruct the volunteer to look at data that may have been collected like the wait times between steps or go back over the observations of the current state notes (Chapter 2). Then have the volunteer report back to the rest of the team where he/she thinks push is being used and improvements can be made. Have them fill out PDSA forms.)

Kanban

Say in your own words: Kanban is a Japanese word that means that a mechanism has been put in place to alert someone to do something. When you go to apply for Social Security (SS) at a SS office, you walk in the door and take a number. When the clerk is ready for the next person, they press a button and your number shows up on a marquis. That is Kanban at work!

Now what does this word Kanban have to do with batching and push and pull? If a pull system is in place, but if the person who is supplying the work (for me to pull) doesn't know I am ready for it, how can he or she make the work available to me in the first place? And when I am done with that piece of work, how can they know when to replenish my "supply" that I can pull from? Kanban comes in here.

Say in your own words: Everyday examples are: in a supermarket using Kanban, when a customer purchases a box of cereal, the supermarket alerts the supplier that a restock item is required. Another example is about reordering bank checks. When you use a checkbook and you are about to run out of checks, there is a reorder slip that appears in the checkbook before you use the last check.

Another example is from the Metro Food Stamp Processing Center Application Process RPI. Numerous phone calls come into the center usually checking on the status of an application. Their call center has indicators that are set up to track number of calls, call wait times and the number of callers in the phone queue. These indicators have a predetermined acceptable threshold. When any threshold is reached, a "pull signal" (a pop-up message on everyone's computers) is sent to get more help in the call center. This is Kanban.

(INSTRUCTIONS: Read aloud the following example from the County Health Clinic Patient Processes RPI:

Things were not running smoothly in the clinic. The receptionist can't leave her workstation because she is the only one working the reception desk. When a client comes in, the receptionist usually calls the nurse who will be seeing the client and either speaks to him/her or leaves a message. Then the receptionist puts the client's chart on the corner of the reception counter for the nurse to see. There are many times that nurses do not get the message, nor do they see the chart waiting for them.

To the RPI team, Kanban would make an improvement. Like so many medical offices these days, every examining room has colored plastic "flags" that usually rest flat on the wall by the door of the exam room. These flags were installed in this county health clinic and used in a unique way. Here is the improvement: when the provider is ready to see the next patient, they flip the white flag out from the wall that is readily seen by the receptionist. Seeing the flag, the receptionist can quickly bring the patient's file to the provider and send the waiting patient down the hall telling them to go to the room with the white flag.)

Takt Time and Balancing the Workload

<u>Say in your own words:</u> Besides solving flow problems with minimal batching, error-proofing, and pull, there is another problem that impedes a

Figure 6.1 Assembly line. Henry Ford's basic idea of flow production is still sound...

smooth flow. It's called an uneven workload. If the workload is not spread out evenly, you will know quickly. Observations and data will show a problem due to a lack of workload balance. If the data one RPI team collected, showed that products and services were not getting to the customer on time, this could be because of the uneven workload. Another RPI team observed some staff sitting idle while others were working hard. This could be an indication that some workers were finished with their work sooner than others and were sitting idle. In the Metro Food Stamp Processing Center RPI, incoming work was placed in separate team buckets to be accessed by each team. Some buckets emptied quicker than others. That meant some teams had little or no work. This was a good example of an uneven workload.

(INSTRUCTIONS: Draw on the flipchart: Processing time. Takt time.)

(Balancing the workload has a technique to it: it involves calculating the processing time at each work station operation. The next step is understanding how fast the pace of the entire process needs to be in order to meet the customer's expectations. This pace is determined by calculating takt time, defined as "the beat of the process flow.")

Say in your own words: Workload balancing means to change the distribution and approach to a series of tasks being completed in order to meet the calculated pace (takt) time of the process. An operator balance chart is a way to show the different work tasks being completed at each phase as compared to takt time. It gives the manager information about where certain tasks may need to be redistributed across work stations.

(INSTRUCTIONS: Hand out: Licensing Process, Step 1 and 2 from Appendix 6.)

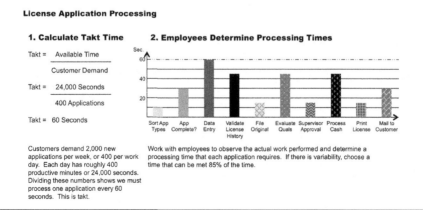

Figure 6.2 Licensing Application Process small version, Steps 1, 2. Each bar is a step in the process

Let's look closely at this chart and see what's on it. Under #1 is listed the formula for calculating takt time. #2 is a bar graph. Each bar represents a work station. And the heights of the bars represent the processing time for tasks in that work station. The dashed horizontal line at the 60-second interval is the takt time. This means one application has to come out of the process every 60 seconds to meet the customer's needs. The chart shows that all tasks are completed at, or below the 60 second mark.

(INSTRUCTIONS: Ask the question, "What can be done if our current processing times do not meet takt time?" You can get them started by giving them a few examples: a) having one person complete more than the one task (merging tasks), b) reducing the batch to only one item, or c) spreading a difficult or time-consuming task across several steps or people.)

Record the team's ideas on the flipchart.

(INSTRUCTIONS: Hand out Licensing Process, Steps 3, 4 and encourage them to read the Self-Study in Appendix 6.)

(You, as the facilitator, will have to take the lead to help the team in balancing the workload, should this improvement recommendation be made. Usually, this improvement gets started after someone calculates the processsing and takt times. The Self-Study in Appendix 6 gives additional steps.

But please note, this balancing workload Self-Study relies on a routine process. Not all government services have such a linear and routine process that lends itself to takt time. In this case, an alternative method to balance the workload may be needed. See the Art of Facilitation for this chapter.)

List of Facilitation Deliverables

- Completed PDSA forms.
- Documented decision to cease batching or minimize it.

The Art of Facilitation: Takt Time May Not Be Our Time

The concept of takt time and balancing the workload can be complex. And often, it is difficult to apply in government mainly because organizational data about demand is often not available. Also, takt time and balancing the workload assumes that there are routine processes and there are people who work on the sequential steps of the workflow, much like an assembly line in a Ford plant. The other challenge is that government has a lot of "knowledge workers." Much of their work goes on in their heads and unless what is going on in their heads, is made explicit to the outside observer, it is difficult to "see" a repetitive process.

The bottom line is this: calculating takt time is challenging in government, not only because of the large number of knowledge workers, but also because there are many provisions of service processes that are not routine with sequential steps. (We did find one for you to study in the Self-Study part of Appendix 6: Lean Colorado gives us an example in their License Application Process and takes you all the way through the solution to balancing your workload.)

One example of service processes that are not routine is in the case in the Field Offices Client Application Process Processes RPI. Clients come to these offices to apply for government benefits. They are served by many different caseworkers who think that linear processes do not apply when working with human problems. The data told the RPI team, that caseworkers did not have time in their schedule to meet clients' needs. The entry point for the clients was not standard: they could come into the branch offices to get services by just dropping in, or come at their appointment time. But for all clients, the wait time to see a caseworker was too long and some clients had to delay receiving benefits. Many clients were scheduled to come back another day. This was a dire situation when people needed food stamps.

These data pointed to a workload that was not balanced. Each worker spent a large amount of time on paperwork, interviewing clients, and making determinations about what programs the clients were eligible for.

An alternative to takt time. The RPI team knew there was tremendous overburden on some caseworkers while others sat idle. That was because every case worker had a different way he/she did the job. Since the team didn't have a visible routine process to observe, there would be no takt time calculation to set the pace for all workers to follow. They had to figure out how to balance the workload by reconfiguring the way the work was done. The team took several time observations of the workers as they interacted with the clients. This helped in determining the average time it would take for certain tasks, such as assessing the client. This resulted in creating a standard cycle time for each worker to perform an assessment for each client. The cycle time could vary, depending on the number of programs for which the client was eligible.

If a client was only eligible for one program, it would take the staff person 20 minutes to process them; for two programs it was 45 minutes; for three it would take 60 minutes. Next, the RPI team recommended that as long as the clients were served, the paperwork could be done another time. Each caseworker would be accountable for how long that took.

All in all, this was their alternative method: they set up a daily work schedule on a big whiteboard for all the staff. From day to day, staff were rotated between duties of seeing clients and completing their required paperwork. (As an added resource, a floating caseworker was assigned each day to see walk-in clients.) The workers had consistency in their work with having sequential client appointments all in one day and a chunk of time to do their paperwork on another day. They were more productive; the clients benefitted from receiving faster service.

FYI:

Figure 6.3 Example: Scheduling board for caseworkers, Field Offices Client Application RPI. Rearranged all staff work so that there was enough time to do required paperwork as well as see clients.

Appendix 6

HANDOUTS:

Error-proof a process

Identify mistakes

What errors/mistakes (defined) occur at each step? (Use the flowchart. Picture each step and think of what goes wrong in its execution. Begin to collect data on errors.)

Identify ways to make procedures less error-prone

Would changing the order of steps prevent mistakes?

Would changing a form prevent mistakes?

Would using a checklist prevent mistakes?

Would clear directions graphically illustrated and prominently display present mistakes?

Can you think of entirely new procedures that are error-proof?

Restructure the work environment

Would changing the work layout prevent any of the mistakes from happening?

Modify current oversight or review methods

Perform successive checks.

Create systems for immediate feedback. Identify abnormalities in the process and where they originated.

Identify mistakes

What errors/mistakes (defined) occur at each step? (Use the flowchart. Picture each step and think of what goes wrong in its execution. Begin to collect data on errors.

I dentify ways to make procedures less error -prone

Would changing the order of steps prevent mistakes?

Would changing a form prevent mistakes?

Would using a checklist prevent mistakes?

Would clear directions graphically illustrated and prominently display present mistakes?

Can you think of entirely new procedures that are error-proof?

Restructure the work environment

Would changing the work layout prevent any of the mistakes from happening?

Modify current oversight or review methods

Perform successive checks.

Create systems for immediate feedback. Identify abnormalities on process and where they originated.

Figure 6.4   Error-proof a process instruction

SELF-STUDY: Balancing workload

License Application Processing

1. Calculate Takt Time

Takt = Available Time
――――――――――
Customer Demand

Takt = 24,000 Seconds
――――――――――
400 Applications

Takt = 60 Seconds

Customers demand 2,000 new applications per week, or 400 per work day. Each day has roughly 400 productive minutes or 24,000 seconds. Dividing these numbers shows we must process one application every 60 seconds. This is takt.

2. Employees Determine Processing Times

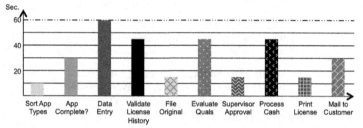

Work with employees to observe the actual work performed and determine a processing time that each application requires. If there is variability, choose a time that can be met 85% of the time.

Figure 6.5　Licensing Process, Steps 1, 2

3. Determine Number of Employees Required

Employees = Total Processing Time
Required ―――――――――――――
Takt

Employees = 310 Seconds per App.
Required ――――――――――――――
60 seconds

Employees = 5.2 Employees to
Required　Process Demand

Based on a total of 310 seconds of processing work for each application, and a takt time of 60 seconds, 5.2 employees are needed to operate this process in balance with demand.

Note: You will need additional employees to cover vacations, etc, but these people should be put to work on other valuable tasks.

4. Combine Tasks to Balance the Work

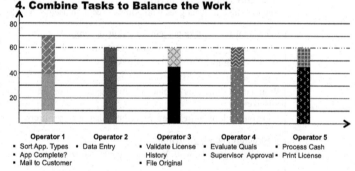

Operator 1	Operator 2	Operator 3	Operator 4	Operator 5
• Sort App. Types	• Data Entry	• Validate License	• Evaluate Quals	• Process Cash
• App Complete?		History	• Supervisor Approval	• Print License
• Mail to Customer		• File Original		

Combine tasks in such a way that each person has work equal to the takt time, and therefore equal to each other. This is not only fair, it ensures that applications will not pile up at any one station. Avoiding these queues improves quality and decreases flow time for each application. This is a recipe for delighting customers!

Note: Cross-train employees to the degree possible so that employees can flex between roles. This keeps people fresh and offers flexibility to your operations.

Figure 6.6　Licensing Chart, Step 3

How to balance the workload.

Remember in Lean, we look at everything from the eyes of the customer. Our processes exist to produce a product or service for the customer. What the customer requires, requests, or expects is called the "demand." View the

License Application Process from Lean Colorado. (Figure 6.6 Licensing Process, Step 1 and 2 and Figure 6.7 Licensing Application Processing, Steps 3, 4.)

Step 1. Calculate takt time. Yes, there is a formula. But it is dependent on data. The organization needs to know the customer's demand: this means determining how much is needed as a product or service during a certain time period. In this example, the organization has data on the number of license applications required in a week. (They must have collected very good historical data to see the trends.) The other unique thing in the formula is that "the time it takes to do the work" is stated in seconds. They figure the workday in hours, then reduce that to minutes, then to seconds. (400 minutes equals about 6.7 hours in the workday allowing for lunch and breaks.) The formula in the example gives us a takt time of 60 seconds. It's important not to confuse takt time with processing time. (Processing time can be thought of as "touch time.") Think of takt time like this...every 60 seconds, a completed application comes out of the process. That's the pace.

Step 2. The next step is pretty straightforward. List the separate tasks in the process and work with the staff to figure out how long it takes to do that task. (This should correspond to whatever you use in the formula...in seconds.) Then you make a bar chart. You add a separate dotted line across the chart that represents the takt time (60 seconds).

Step 3. The next step is pretty interesting because it goes straight to finding out how many people you need to do the work in the process. Again, a simple formula which requires calculating the total processing time. Add up all the times of the different bars on the chart. That is 310 seconds. Divide that by the takt (60) and you get 5.2 employees.

The last step (4) requires you to figure out how to have only 5.2 employees and get an application through the process every 60 seconds. In this case, the tasks are combined. First you make a new chart called the operator's chart. Just label the "X" axis with 5 operators and "Y" axis in 20 second increments. Now combine tasks that add up to the takt line. (You will notice that the first operator's task does exceed takt time (that's where the

0.2 staff comes in.)) This will work because one of the tasks (mail to customer) is at the end of the process.

Here is another example from the book, *Everything I Know About Lean I Learned in the First Grade* by Robert Martichenko.* Here was a different case of getting all the schoolchildren through the lunch line in a specific time period. The lunchroom manager figured out his takt time and knew he couldn't meet it given the staff he had. He also couldn't extend the lunch time period. What did he do?

> …he timed the students at the cash register step….it took 18 seconds…this created a bottleneck. Couldn't get them to do it faster….so he added another register. Two children at a time entering into the cash register. Better to buy a new register than the other option of extending the lunch hour. Knowing the beat helps him to plan other things: the right number of employees to staff the line, buying the right amount of food, knowing exactly when to move more food from the freezer to the shelves.
>
> **(Martichenko 2012, pp. 12–13)**

* Martichenko, Robert (2012). *Everything I Know About Lean I Learned in the First Grade* Boston, MA: Lean Enterprise Institute.

Chapter 7

Smooth Out the Flow:
Improve How the Work Is Performed

Why Bother with Standardization? What Is It?

<u>Say in your own words:</u> In Lean, if our goal is to provide expected services to our customer, the presence of variation in the process is a problem. Variation is when the same work is performed from one person to another, but each person does it differently. This can cause a different level of service and delivery for the same product from one customer to the next. What's needed is standardization.

What is it? Standardized work is not about procedure statements or work rules documentation. It is about getting the people who are doing the work to agree to do it the same way. The workers use standards: the same sequence, method, time, and number of tasks to complete a given process.

How Do You Put Standardization in Place?

Standardization is implemented by the people who do the work. As a group, they define the who, what (how), when, and where the work is to be performed. It includes training, workspace standardization, storage, walkways, signage, file organization and standardized (and, of course, streamlined) forms. There are tools to help depict and display standards.

(INSTRUCTIONS: Draw the tools on the flipchart.)

> **List of Standardization Tools**
>
> - templates
> - checklists
> - file management protocols
> - scheduled meetings and meeting management protocols office and workstation configuration
> - communication protocols
> - consolidation of forms, orders, etc.
> - electronic data transfer (vs manual)

Figure 7.1   Standardization tools

<u>Say in your own words:</u> (pointing to the flipchart) these are some of the tools used to facilitate standardizing work. Can any of you think of anymore? (Put their answers on the flipchart.)

(INSTRUCTIONS: Read aloud examples from RPIs that have been successfully completed.)

This example is from the Older Americans Act (OAA) Allocation Process RPI. In the OAA RPI flowchart, there was a step labelled "compute the formula." This step was important to the process because it meant the state office computes the formula for allocating the amount of funds for each field office. The problem was that there was no consistency in using the suggested formula. In fact, different offices were inputting factors into their own formulas based on their interpretation of the federal regulation. This created different levels of allocation to the local offices and there were a lot of complaints. *(As the facilitator, it is up to you to question assumptions. Sending some of the RPI team to read and analyze the federal regulations gave them needed information. They concluded that the cause of the problem was that there was a lot of "wiggle room" in the clarity of the regulation which made it subject to various interpretations and practices.)*

(INSTRUCTIONS: Hand out the Code of Federal Regulations from Appendix 7.)

Code of Federal Regulations (Title 45, Vol. 4)
(Revised as of October 1, 2002)
From the U.S. Government Printing Office via GPO Process
(Cite: 45CFR1321.37)

(Page 236)

TITLE 45—PUBLIC WELFARE
CHAPTER XIII—OFFICE OF HUMAN DEVELOPMENT SERVICES, DEPARTMENT OF HEALTH AND
HUMAN SERVICES

PART 1321—GRANTS TO STATE AND COMMUNITY PROGRAMS ON AGING—Table of Contents

Subpart B—State Agency Responsibilities

Sec. 1321.37 Intrastate funding formula.

(a) The State agency, after consultation with all area agencies in the State, shall develop and use an intrastate funding formula for the allocation of funds to area agencies under this part. The State agency shall publish the formula for review and comment by older persons, other appropriate agencies and organizations and the general public. The formula shall reflect the proportion among the planning and service areas of persons age 60 and over in greatest economic or social need with particular attention to low-income minority individuals. The State agency shall review and update its formula as often as a new State plan is submitted for approval.

(b) The intrastate funding formula shall provide for a separate allocation of funds received under section 303 (f) for preventive health services. In the award of such funds to selected planning and service areas, the State agency shall give priority to areas of the State:
(1) Which are medically underserved; and
(2) In which there are large numbers of individuals who have the greatest economic and social need for such services.
(c) The State agency shall submit its intrastate formula to the Commissioner for review and comment. The intrastate formula shall be submitted separately from the State plan.

Figure 7.2   Code of Federal Regulations pertaining to calculating formulas, OAA Allocation Process RPI

(Read aloud.) The **solution** was to bring field offices together to agree on a new standard formula to use.

Say in your own words: Here is another example from the East Metro Food Stamp Intake Process RPI. Let me read you an excerpt from their written report:

(Read aloud.) RECEPTIONIST

Receptionists' processes are inconsistent from station to station.

There are four receptionists. Each receptionist does his/her work differently.

Receptionists' scheduling processes is cumbersome and results in inefficient work.

The physical space where the receptionists' work is inefficient and cluttered.

Traffic pattern for receptionists behind the desk is crowded and things that each receptionist may need are not readily at hand.

Reception area is cluttered with notices all over the wall that are not conducive to a friendly customer-service environment.

The wait area in front of the receptionists is overcrowded and many times, clients do not have chairs to sit on. The longer the clients wait, the more agitated they become.

Ask: What do you think the RPI team did to standardize the reception duties and area? (INSTRUCTIONS: Record answers on flipchart. Discuss.)

Say in your own words: This next example is not from an RPI, but from the Public Health National Accreditation Board. Its members developed standards through the use of performance measures. These measures are to be adhered to by state and county health departments.

(INSTRUCTION: Write on flipchart: https://phaboard.org.)

This whole system's intent is to provide uniform services, information, and training throughout the entire system. When this is achieved, one county's health department will have the same level of service and quality as any other county's health department. Take a look at the website on the flipchart.

Pig Exercise Instructions

1. Draw a letter M at the top left intersection. Bottom center of M touches the intersection.

2. Draw the letter W at the bottom left intersection. Top center of W touches the intersection.

3. Draw the letter W at the bottom right intersection. Top center of W touches the intersection.

4. Draw an arc from the letter M to the top right intersection.

5. Draw another arc from the top right intersection to the bottom right W.

6. Draw an arc between the two bottom W's.

7. Draw the letter O in the center left box.

8. Draw an arc from the letter M to the tangent of the circle.

9. Draw an arc from the left W to the tangent of the of the circle.

10. Draw an arc for the eye. Half way between M and circle.

11. Draw an arc for the mouth. Half way between W and circle.

12. Draw the cursive letter e near the top of the arc on the right.

13. And finally draw two dots in the middle of the circle for the pig's nose.

Figure 7.3 Pig Exercise Instructions

TEACHING EXERCISE

(INSTRUCTION: Hand out: Instructions for the Pig Exercise and blank graph paper from Appendix 7.)

Say in your own words: These are the instructions for this exercise. I am the customer and you are the makers of the product. I would like you to take the instructions for drawing a pig and draw the pig on the graph paper. You have 20 minutes. When you are finished, please tape your pig up on the wall so that we can see them. *(When the team sees all the differences, they will begin to understand the lack of clarity in the instructions. They will see each person's interpretation of the instructions and ultimately realize the need for standardization.)*

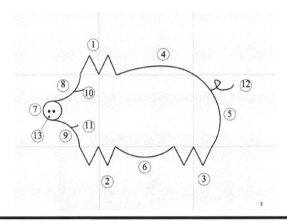

Figure 7.4   The correct way to draw a pig

<u>Say in your own words:</u> As the customer, I am not very happy. This is not what I wanted. (Point out all the variations in the pictures.) Now I am going to give you a picture of a pig that is drawn the correct way.

(INSTRUCTIONS: Hand out the Pig Exercise Answer from Appendix 7.)

Show Me How to Do It: Facilitation Case Study from Field Offices Client Application Process RPI

<u>Say in your own words:</u> Your job as an RPI team, is to understand what is standardization and how it is important. During an RPI, improvements are made to a process and the tasks to do the work in that new process need to be standardized. Here is an example of how standardization came about from an RPI team that was able to get agreement among three different branch offices to do their new work in a standard way.

Before the RPI, all branch offices did their work differently, so much do that the number of steps and the time it took for the process varied from one branch office to another.

Here's the problem:

When the manager of a region asked for this RPI, the caseworkers in all three of her branches were doing the same work but were all doing it differently. She was concerned. The manager knew that variation eats up time and resources. She also worried about capacity of the staff to do all this work. This proved valid' Recently the state legislature passed more new programs that had to be implemented by the staff in the field. This would add to the workload of the caseworkers, yet there was no provision for an increase in staff. Here was the solution: the manager felt that standardization was a way to streamline the work and thus free up time for workers.

The following case study describes the steps the facilitator took to guide the RPI team through the method of standardization.

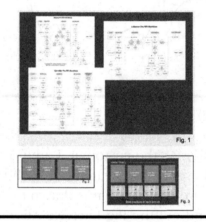

Figure 7.5 Figure 1: Each office did it differently

(INSTRUCTIONS: Hand out: Case Study Figures 1, 2, 3 (one page) from Appendix 7.)

1. Facilitator displayed all flowcharts

This is what the facilitator did first. The facilitator taped all the flowcharts on the wall for all the RPI team to see. This is Figure 1 on your handout.

These are the different flowcharts from each branch office for the same process. Each office recorded the number of steps in the process. A timeline across the bottom of each chart showed how long the flow of work took. This display convinced the RPI team that there was a lot of variation in their work.

2. Needed to step back from details to form big picture

Refer to Figure 2 on your handout. Next, the facilitator asked the team to put aside their flowcharts and take a step back. In order to get them out of the weeds and work towards standardization, the facilitator asked the question, "What is the body of work that you do in all these flowcharts?"

The team was able to boil their work down to four major steps. These were considered the essential steps in their work with clients. *(You might think of this as going back to the level of developing a value stream.)*

<u>3. Facilitator led team to share best practices to get to standardization</u>
<u>Say:</u> refer to Figure 3 on your handout.

The next step for the facilitator was to move the RPI team towards the development of standards. The facilitator asked the team to go to the wall where the four major steps were written and put up their own best practices with sticky notes under each major step. *(The team of workers had to decide what they are "shooting for" since they all do it a little differently. How do they make the decision for the "best way to standardize?" The Lean answer is to find out who does it the best among them (most efficient, few errors) and adopt that as a standard step. In the meantime, the facilitator urged them to investigate "best practices" in similar organizations (e.g., other states) if they needed a reference.)*

The facilitator then asked the team to dialogue with each other about the sticky notes of "best ways." The team negotiated with each other to adopt some best practices over others. This brought them a step closer to standardized work. Here is another handout. This is a list of best practices in each branch created by the RPI team.

(INSTRUCTIONS: Hand out "What Works Best in Each Branch," Appendix 7.)

<u>4. Facilitator led team to develop one flowchart</u>

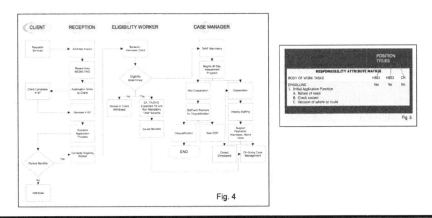

Figure 7.6 Case Study Figures 4, 5

(INSTRUCTIONS: Hand out Case Study, Figures 4, 5.
and refer to Figure 4 on your handout.)

The facilitator asked the RPI team to develop a new flowchart the best they could, using the information from the work they had done so far.

The facilitator realized that the RPI team had a gnawing question. The problem was this: could the staff, with their prescriptive government job descriptions, be constrained from doing the new tasks in the new process that were required? This was a new challenge for the facilitator. The facilitator had to help the team answer this question. They needed to change their paradigm about job descriptions.

Then the facilitator used the flipchart instead of handouts. From Figure 7.8, the facilitator drew the bottom triangle labelled Job Description.

Figure 7.7 Triangles

5. <u>Facilitator helps team to change their paradigm</u>
Sometimes, without realizing it, the facilitator told the team, we do things backwards. We let the job descriptions dictate the work to be done rather than first asking, "What's the job that needs to be done?" (Then the facilitator drew on the same flipchart the second triangle labelled "Job Needing to Be Done" to overlap on the first triangle.) The facilitator then asked the team: "Is it possible that the current job descriptions will support our new process? If not, what can we do?"

6. <u>Facilitator led team to cross-walk new tasks to old job descriptions</u>
The facilitator let the RPI Team take the lead. The team knew what to do next. This is what they did: They matched up the new tasks the staff would have to do with their job descriptions.

For example, they retrieved the job descriptions of Human Services Specialist 1 (HSS1), Human Services Specialist 3 (HSS3) and Case Manager (CM) and studied them thoroughly. They analyzed these to see where there were mandatory tasks and where there was some flexibility.

Refer to Figure 5 on your case study handout (the Responsibility Attribute Matrix).

The team used this project management tool, the Responsibility Attribute Matrix, to help them in their analysis. They listed the new tasks in the new standardized process on the left of the matrix and then, across the top of the matrix, they put the initials (e.g., HSS1) for the current staff positions. Then they cross-walked the two.

In Figure 5, as you can see on the left of the matrix there are the Enrolling Tasks that were crossed-walked to the positions on the right. The position had a "yes" by it indicating that they could do these new tasks given their current job descriptions. *(When the regional manager requested the RPI, she originally wondered whether more of the administrative assistants could take over some of the work of the caseworkers. This proved true when the team matched the HSS 1 position (an admin assistance position), to new tasks.)*

List of Facilitation Deliverables

- PDSA Forms.
- Standards documentation.

The Art of Facilitation: Knowledge Workers (The Professional Bureaucracy)

Government and non-profit operations look nothing like an assembly line in an automotive plant. This is what some call the machine bureaucracy. Instead of machinists, government has a lot of knowledge workers. Henry Minzberg referred to them as the Professional Bureaucracy*. Knowledge work involves expertise and judgment that depends heavily on tacit knowledge. When trying to understand the work in the process, knowledge work is a challenge to mapping the process.

The key is to interview the knowledge worker and elicit from them the routine steps that they follow. For instance, ask the knowledge worker, "You arrived at a decision you make routinely. What are the steps, both mental and physical, that you go through to arrive at that decision?" These steps can be mapped and analyzed. The flowchart identifies that knowledge work includes many routine actions that don't involve judgment or expertise and can eat up huge amounts of time. Examples: simple routines such as printing documents, requesting information (needed to make a decision), and setting up meetings.

> 1. "Doing the work all the same way limits my creativity."
>
> 2. "I deal with people not machines. Therefore, I must be flexible".

Figure 7.8   Quotes from Staff

Don't be fooled when knowledge workers use excuses (like the ones below) for not documenting their work in a flowchart or saying their work (or parts of it) can't be standardized.

*Machine bureaucracy** emphasizes the authority of the hierarchical nature/structure which **can** be called reliance on the power of office while **professional bureaucracy** emphasizes the authority of a profession or the power of expertise. (Henry Mintzberg, 1992)

Appendix 7

HANDOUTS:

Code of Federal Regulations (Title 45, Vol. 4)
(Revised as of October 1, 2002)
From the U.S. Government Printing Office via GPO Process
(Cite: 45CFR1321.37)

(Page 236)

TITLE 45---PUBLIC WELFARE
CHAPTER XIII—OFFICE OF HUMAN DEVELOPMENT SERVICES, DEPARTMENT OF HEALTH AND
HUMAN SERVICES

PART 1321—GRANTS TO STATE AND COMMUNITY PROGRAMS ON AGING—Table of Contents

Subpart B—State Agency Responsibilities

Sec. 1321.37 Intrastate funding formula.

(a) The State agency, after consultation with all area agencies in the State, shall develop and use an intrastate funding formula for the allocation of funds to area agencies under this part. The State agency shall publish the formula for review and comment by older persons, other appropriate agencies and organizations and the general public. The formula shall reflect the proportion among the planning and service areas of persons age 60 and over in greatest economic or social need with particular attention to low-income minority individuals. The State agency shall review and update its formula as often as a new State plan is submitted for approval.

(b) The intrastate funding formula shall provide for a separate allocation of funds received under section 303 (f) for preventive health services. In the award of such funds to selected planning and service areas, the State agency shall give priority to areas of the State:
(1) Which are medically underserved; and
(2) In which there are large numbers of individuals who have the greatest economic and social need for such services.
(c) The State agency shall submit its intrastate formula to the Commissioner for review and comment. The intrastate formula shall be submitted separately from the State plan.

Figure 7.9   OAA Allocation Process RPI formula

Pig Exercise Instructions

1. Draw a letter M at the top left intersection. Bottom center of M touches the intersection.

2. Draw the letter W at the bottom left intersection. Top center of W touches the intersection.

3. Draw the letter W at the bottom right intersection. Top center of W touches the intersection.

4. Draw an arc from the letter M to the top right intersection.

5. Draw another arc from the top right intersection to the bottom right W.

6. Draw an arc between the two bottom W's.

7. Draw the letter O in the center left box.

8. Draw an arc from the letter M to the tangent of the circle.

9. Draw an arc from the left W to the tangent of the of the circle.

10. Draw an arc for the eye. Half way between M and circle.

11. Draw an arc for the mouth. Half way between W and circle.

12. Draw the cursive letter e near the top of the arc on the right.

13. And finally draw two dots in the middle of the circle for the pig's nose.

Figure 7.10   Pig Exercise Instructions

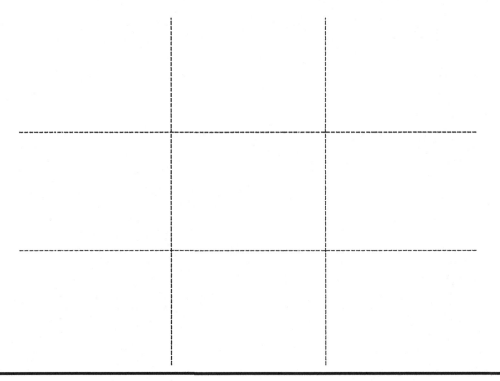

Figure 7.11   Blank Graph Paper

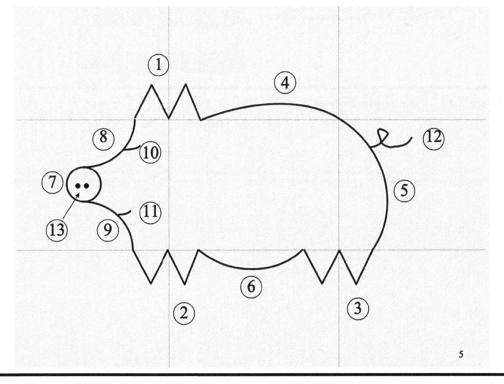

Figure 7.12   Pig Answer

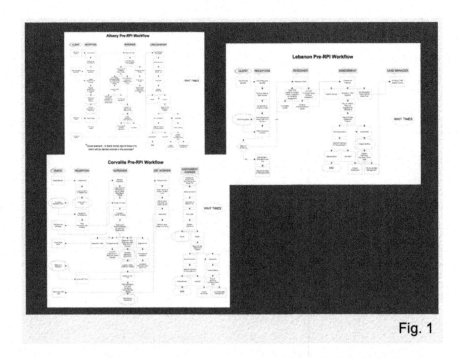

Fig. 1

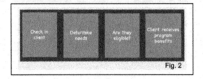

Fig. 2

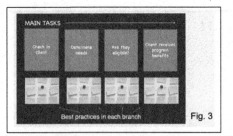

Fig. 3

Figure 7.13   Case Study, Figures 1, 2, 3

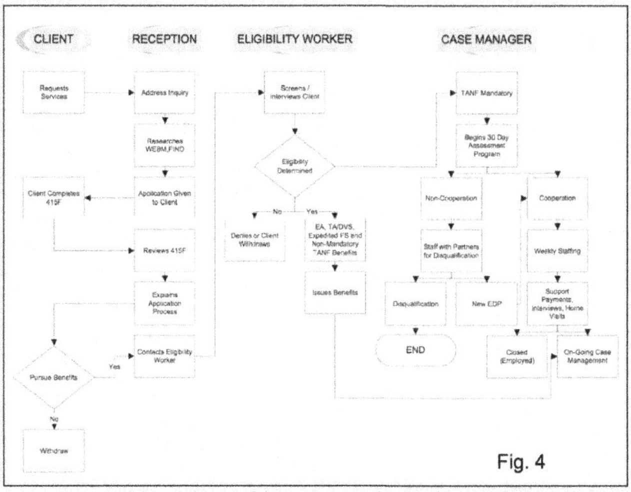

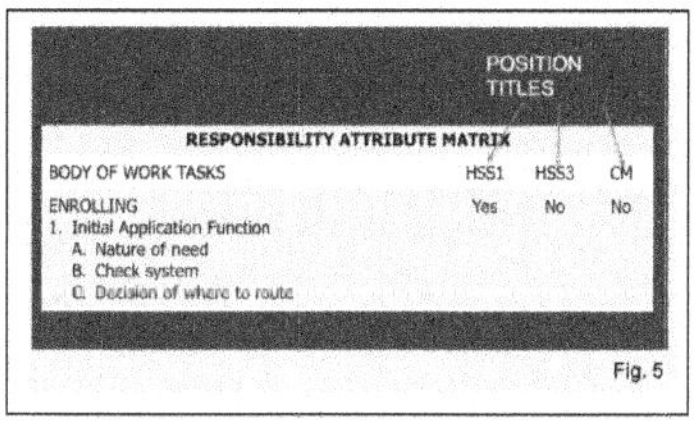

Figure 7.14   Case Study, Figures 4, 5

What works best in each branch?

PROCESS STEP: Reception and check in

Forms

Location of the locked file cabinet-vouchers, etc. Review of Application/Documentation

Obtain copies of essential info "I" drive for appts, assessments

Communication Reception / Workers Mail Distribution. (Corvallis also) Review of OHP/MAA

Coordination of support staff

Bi-weekly support staff meetings

Having phone receptionist (less distractions at reception) Calling for case transfers

Client/Receptionist relationship

PROCESS STEP: Assessment

Being seen by assessment specialist, having a uniform PDP Having partners & classes in branch

Daily monitoring of attendance Daily/Weekly staffing

Keeping JAS updated

Having scheduled appointments for assessment workers Hold client accountable

Daily contact w/client (go in classroom/attendance) Weekly staffing w/partners

Good assessment of need for support services

Figure 7.15   **What works best in each branch, Field Offices Client Application Process RPI**

SELF-STUDY: Documentation tool for Standard Work

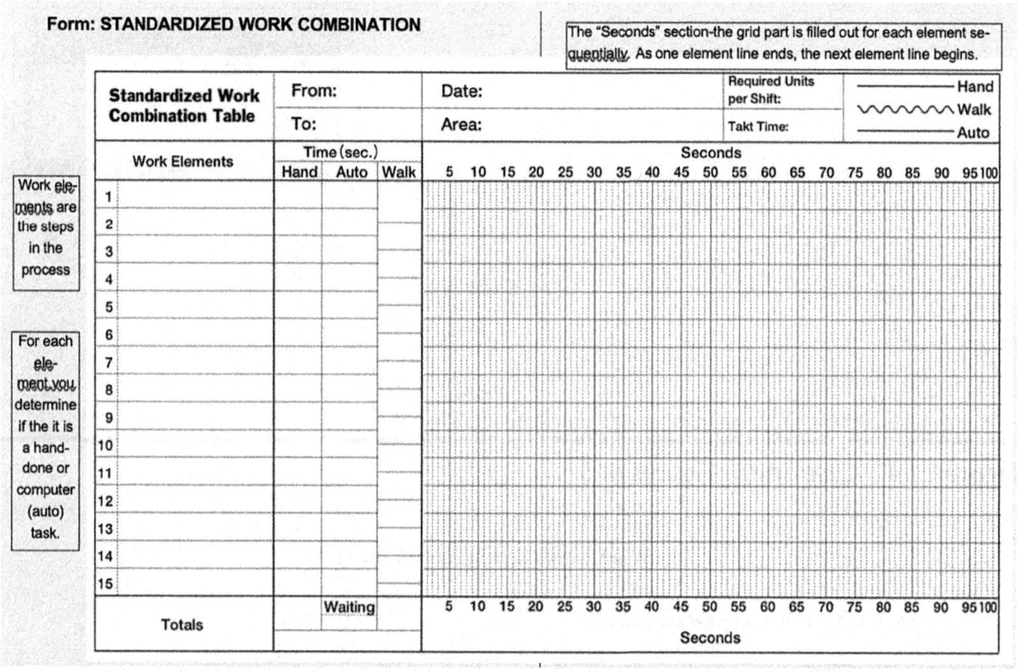

Form: STANDARDIZED WORK COMBINATION

The "Seconds" section-the grid part is filled out for each element sequentially. As one element line ends, the next element line begins.

Work elements are the steps in the process

For each element you determine if the it is a hand-done or computer (auto) task.

Standardized Work Combination Table	From:	Date:	Required Units per Shift:	——— Hand
	To:	Area:	Takt Time:	∿∿∿ Walk ——— Auto

Work Elements	Time (sec.) Hand	Auto	Walk	Seconds 5 10 15 20 25 30 35 40 45 50 55 60 65 70 75 80 85 90 95 100
1				
2				
3				
4				
5				
6				
7				
8				
9				
10				
11				
12				
13				
14				
15				
Totals		Waiting		5 10 15 20 25 30 35 40 45 50 55 60 65 70 75 80 85 90 95 100 Seconds

Figure 7.16 Form used for standard work determination

Chapter 8

Smooth Out the Flow: *Improve the Process Supports*

Mini-Lecture: Overview of Supports

<u>Say in your own words:</u> This chapter is unique to this manual. It's included because RPI teams often overlook supports when developing their improvement recommendations. Supports are the materials, the equipment, the environment that are integral to our processes. For instance, we forget that new forms may need to be developed to implement an improvement, or that reconfiguring the workspace improves the work flow.

Here is a quick overview.

(INSTRUCTIONS: On the flipchart, write as a list: Materials. Environment. Equipment.)

Handout: Questions to ask about supports

MATERIALS: forms, templates, reports, etc.

Are the forms, templates, macros, software, reports that a worker uses to perform their tasks adequate and serve its purpose?

ENVIRONMENT: physical and cultural

Does the physical space where the work is being done support the flow? Environment is the location, and the space where work is being done.

Do work teams sit near one another? And are cells set up of team members and set up in such a way that there the work setup follows how the product or service goes through the process.

EQUIPMENT: hardware, phone systems, printers, etc.

Are the workers using the latest equipment or are they using a tired legacy system?

If there are many systems, do they talk to each other?

Are there enough printers for the workers?

Do the fax machines work?

Figure 8.1   Questions to ask about supports

(INSTRUCTIONS: Hand out: Questions to ask about supports, from Appendix 8.)

Say: This handout asks questions about supports that you should know. Let's read it through. *(Give them enough time to read all the questions.)*

Does anyone need clarification before we see examples?

Materials

(INSTRUCTIONS: On the flipchart, write as a list: Materials: Forms, Formulas, Macros.)

Forms

(INSTRUCTIONS: Hand out photo of flowcharts and forms.)

Figure 8.2   39 forms in the process, Child Welfare Case Transfer Process RPI

Say in your own words: This is about materials, specifically forms. This handout shows a flowchart (made up of well-placed sticky notes) from the Child Welfare Case Transfer Process RPI. At the bottom of the flowchart are taped up all 39 forms (both official and unofficial) used in that process.

An obvious improvement would be to reduce the number of forms. This is how the RPI team did it.

(INSTRUCTIONS: Read aloud the following recommendation from the Child Welfare Case Transfer Process RPI.)

R18. Recommendation: Reduce the number of forms.

1. Lay all forms out on a table.
2. Sort out the official from the unofficial forms.
3. Examine all the unofficial forms. Make a list of the fields of information that show up on more than one form.

4. Now make a list of fields on the unofficial forms that are unique, that only show up on one form and not others. Determine whether these are fields required by federal or state policy. If so, they will be included on a new unofficial form. If not, determine if a new form needs to be developed or added to an official form.
5. Start creating a new unofficial form. First, put the required fields on this new form from step 4. Second, add the other fields from the list in step 3.
6. For fields of information that are not on the new informal form, may sure that there are other created forms that have the unique fields that are needed by some of the staff.
7. Count the number of forms now needed. Compare to the original amount!
8. Send in a request to the agency forms office to update their formal forms in order to decrease the reliance on informal forms.

Formulas

Say in your own words: Formulas are part of materials supports.

Remember this example where a formula nearly got overlooked as a support. It was from the Older Americans Act (OAA) Allocation Process RPI. This RPI was requested because the local field federal offices of the Agency on Aging were concerned about their budgets. Their budgets, shown on spreadsheets, were made up of federal monies that were passed down to the state government offices, who in turn, distributed them to their local field offices. The amount of monies allocated to the local field offices was determined by a formula, developed from criteria advised by federal policy.

In this RPI, the team discovered the use of an errant formula while analyzing some budget spreadsheets and saw discrepancies that led them to ask the Five Why's. Due to the structure of any Excel spreadsheet, the details are hidden. The details were not discovered for a long time resulting in an overallocation of federal funds over 2-year periods.

The staff person who created the spreadsheet had left the organization so the RPI team had no one to interview to get more details.

Macros

Say in your own words: Here is an example of macros as a part of materials support.

In the OHP Processing Center RPI, the RPI team recorded time observations of all the eligibility workers. Eligibility workers perform the same tasks, yet the team found variations from one worker to another, in the length of time to complete a task. For example, one worker took 40 minutes; another worker took 8 minutes. Why? The team discovered that the "8-minute-worker" had developed a macro for her desktop that made her work go faster. (Talk about a best practice!) The team recommended that this macro be put on everyone's desktop.

Environment

Cultural Environment

(INSTRUCTIONS: On the flipchart, write as a list:
Environment: Cultural, Physical.)

(INSTRUCTIONS: Read aloud from the handout, Questions to ask about supports: (Environment): "Does the culture of the organization support improvement?")

Say in your own words: Here is a way to define a cultural environment: it represents the values of the organization.

Or put in a more specific way, "Is there a culture in the organization that promotes and retains Lean as a model for management?" *(Here is an example: When recruiting staff to be on the RPI team, getting their supervisor to approve their time away from their daily job is part of the cultural environment support you need. If there is hesitation, make sure you listen to supervisors' concerns and offer suggestions. Aside from mentioning how short the commitment is ("It will be over before you know it!"), emphasize the benefits to the supervisor such as the RPI team member will bring back new learnings and tools to share with the rest of the staff.)*

A supportive culture is foundational to continuous improvement in an organization (which is covered as a topic in Chapter 10).

Physical Environment

(INSTRUCTIONS: On the flipchart, write as a list:

Physical Environment: Teams sit near each other.
Tools, etc. close to the work.
Use visual management.)

(INSTRUCTIONS: Read aloud from the handout, Questions to ask about supports: "Does the physical space where the work is being done support the flow?")

<u>Say in your own words:</u> Are work stations and supply areas close to where the work is being done? Or is a lot of time wasted in walking and movement by staff to get what they need?

The space should be organized to replicate how the process flows and to locate the tools near where the work is. Here is how to do it.

APPENDIX C.1: NUMBER OF FOOTSTEPS

	STEPS 0201
	10 Steps from Reception to Screener Desk
	10 Steps from Screener Desk to Reception to pick up client
	10 Steps from Lobby back to Screener Desk
	10 Steps from Screener Desk to Reception for Assessment Log
SCREENING	10 Steps from Reception back to Screener Desk
	10 Steps from Reception back to Screener Desk
	25 Steps from Screener Desk to Open Case Retrieval
	25 Steps from Open Case back to Screener Desk
	10 Steps from Screener Desk to Reception Bucket
ASSESSMENT	15 Steps to deliver file to ASW
	15 Steps from ASW to pick up client
	15 Steps from Lobby to ASW desk
	20 Steps from ASW desk to Copier / Printer

Figure 8.3   Counting the footsteps in the process, OHP Processing Center Application Process

<u>Teams sit near each other</u>

Move the workers closer together. There often is unnecessary time and money spent trying to accomplish work by the people who routinely work together. The handout shows you why this is a good idea.

(INSTRUCTIONS: Hand out Counting Steps from Appendix 8.)

<u>Say in your own words:</u> This handout shows simple data, just counting the distance between work stations from the Oregon Health Plan Processing Center Application Process RPI. This is the first step in making improvements.

And in Chapter 2, we reviewed another costing out example from East Metro Food Stamp Intake Process RPI.

These examples counted the number of footsteps from work station to work station to provide documentation for a needed improvement.

<u>Tools, equipment, floor markings close to the work</u>

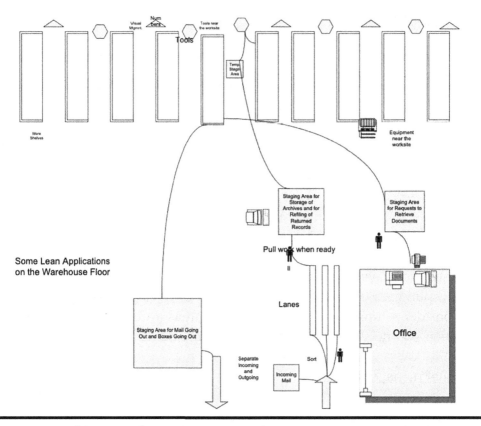

Figure 8.4   Archives Warehouse Storage Process RPI

Say in your own words: Also in Chapter 2, the floorplan mini-group marked up a blueprint of the work area. They identified teams of workers, and marked the location of printers, copiers and faxes. Some were located far away from where the work was being done. The improvement recommendation was to move the equipment closer to where the work was being performed.

(INSTRUCTIONS: Hand out the Archives RPI floorplan of storage warehouse from Appendix 8.)

Say in your own words: Here is an example from the Archives RPI. The Archives warehouse floor area is a square block. This is what you would see in the warehouse: workers storing boxes of files and documents and workers retrieving them from storage (usually from high shelves for which they need to use a forklift), all the while moving back and forth from the loading dock.

Many times, the workers have to go hunt for the tools they need such as a cutter to open boxes. This interrupts their work and moves them away from the location where they are working.

Other things you would see in the warehouse is the chaos on the loading dock. There are boxes coming into the warehouse to be stored, all mixed in with boxes going out of the warehouse to be delivered to people who requested them. Clear floor markings would be helpful in separating out the incoming from the outgoing.

(INSTRUCTIONS: Read aloud – This is a recommendation from the Archives Warehouse Storage Process RPI Report:

- Put office in a place that is central to the work needing to be done.
- Organize equipment near where the work is being done. (No retracing of steps to get a cutting knife.)
- Reorganize the loading dock with markings to separate out incoming from outgoing.
- Instead of having no control over incoming work, put work in "lanes" and pull the next piece of work instead of having it pushed on you.
- Consider setting up temporary staging areas around the warehouse when you need to get in and out of some boxes often.)

Use visual management

Figure 8.5 Team buckets that hold work to be done, OHP Processing Center Application Process RPI

<u>Say in your own words:</u> Setting up visual management in a work area can be a great improvement. Visual management aims to make the physical situation easily understood merely by looking at it. We saw this with the Archives RPI example when tape was put on the warehouse floor for separating out incoming/outgoing storage boxes.

The goal of visual management is to display information so that when someone sees it, they understand the information instantly.

(INSTRUCTIONS: Hand out photo of team buckets from Appendix 8.)

<u>Say in your own words:</u> Here is an example from the OHP Processing Center Application Process RPI. (We saw this used as an example in balancing the workload.) There are file buckets displayed prominently in a central place containing the work for each work team. The file buckets are labelled with the team name: North, South, East, and West. A manager can quickly look at the buckets and see the work progress of each team by the number of files in the bucket. When one team has very few files, the manager can move some of that team to assist other teams.

<u>Say in your own words:</u> Another version of visual management is the display of large performance boards (which will be covered in Chapter 10.) This can display metrics of the work team as well as messages of progress from the manager to the staff. After RPI's are completed, many managers put up implementation goals on a huge white board to report to all staff such as: "…our backlog is 50% less today" or "We are making progress towards reducing how many days to produce one application; last week it was 20 days, this week, 15 days."

Equipment

(INSTRUCTIONS: On the flipchart, write as a list: Equipment: IT Hardware, Office Equipment.)

Figure 8.6   Equipment

What Is Needed for Our Daily Work

<u>Say in your own words:</u> IT hardware and office equipment are used in our daily work. Are they a help or a hindrance?

Here is an example about equipment from the Foster Care Certification Process RPI. In this RPI, caseworkers were often out of the office (and away from their computers) either making home visits, conducting face-to-face interviews, or appearing in court. When out of the office, they wrote their notes by hand and filled out forms manually. Then they came back to the office and added, by hand, more detail to their notes and forms. Lastly, they were required to input all information and forms into their computer. Often, staff worked late to complete their paperwork.

The RPI team recommended that laptops be purchased for all caseworkers to take on their assignments outside of the office.

(INSTRUCTIONS: Read aloud from the PDSA Form: "A caseworker will utilize a laptop or similar technology during contacts with clients on a trial basis of 4–5 weeks. The laptop needs to include all the forms, including release of information forms, all criminal record checks, and adoption assistance applications. The laptop would need to have the stylus that the RPI team discussed, so clients could sign the form on the computer. Central Office would need to accept computer-generated and signed forms. The RPI team would need the flexibility to use the current NCR (National Cash Register) paper form or the electronic forms, depending on the location and circumstances.")

What Is Needed from Our IT Systems

<u>Say in your own words:</u> Sometimes our hardware doesn't keep up with the kind of assistance we need when doing our work. *(Whenever you are facilitating, note these types of problems: old systems that can't support multiple applications and delays because the technology just doesn't have the "fire power.")*

The first example occurred when the OHP Processing Center RPI team was observing workers checking the income of someone applying for a health card: The team couldn't figure out why one step in the process was taking so long. They decided to conduct a Five Why's Exercise which led them to the answer.

(INSTRUCTIONS: Read aloud.

"Why does the income step take so long?"
"Because we have instructions that tell us we have to check many different databases."
"Why does checking many different databases affect the time?"
"Because we have to print off every screen of each database."
"Why do you have to print off each screen of each database?"

"Because the system doesn't allow flexible toggling between different databases.")

(This example only got to the "third why question" and the solution was obvious: they needed to figure out how to get the various databases to work together. This was a request that was submitted to the IT Support Desk to fix.)

Here is an example from the Metro Food Stamp RPI adding time to the process, not shortening it:

(INSTRUCTIONS: Read aloud.

- Inability to transfer a case from a branch and then Set Up, Pend, Approve, or Deny It on the same day. Time is lost because the transfer request into the eligibility tracking system does not take effect until the next day (batch processed).
- There is a wait of 24 hours to barcode due to a default "received date" in the DB2 (Database 2) program used by the mailroom/barcoding.
- There is no standard word processing software; some employees have MS Word and others have Corel.
- Old PCs do not have enough memory to support multiple applications open at one time. (Having multiple applications open at one time is needed to allow for cutting and pasting between systems.))

IT Systems: Automate manual steps where possible

Say in your own words: Sometimes our hardware can be enhanced to support a process, such as automating manual steps when possible.

In the Financial Services Budgetary Process RPI, the RPI team developed a flowchart to understand the work flow of "Transferring Treasury Funds to the General Funds." Nobody had ever documented this before and therefore no one knew the many manual steps the worker had to perform daily. This worker had to operate under a tight deadline. All of these steps had to be completed before she could enter information into the electronic Financial System. Other operations relied on her completing her tasks first before they could do theirs. Seeing the new flowchart, management saw the complexity of the manual tasks and readily approved a work order to have the manual steps be automated. *(Often in government, this is what happens: staff are always working 'behind the eight ball' and they do what they have to do to get the job done!)*

List of Facilitation Deliverables

- Completed PDSA forms.
- Information and documentation of each support improvement.

Appendix 8

HANDOUTS:

Handout: Questions to ask about supports

MATERIALS: forms, templates, reports, etc.

Are the forms, templates, macros, software, reports that a worker uses to perform their tasks adequate and serve its purpose?

ENVIRONMENT: physical and cultural

Does the physical space where the work is being done support the flow? Environment is the location, and the space where work is being done.

Do work teams sit near one another? And are cells set up of team members and set up in such a way that there the work setup follows how the product or service goes through the process.

EQUIPMENT: hardware, phone systems, printers, etc.

Are the workers using the latest equipment or are they using a tired legacy system?

If there are many systems, do they talk to each other?

Are there enough printers for the workers?

Do the fax machines work?

Figure 8.7   Questions to ask

Figure 8.8   Flowchart with Forms Child Welfare Case Transfer Process RPI

APPENDIX C.1: NUMBER OF FOOTSTEPS

STEPS 0201

	10 Steps from Reception to Screener Desk
	10 Steps from Screener Desk to Reception to pick up client
	10 Steps from Lobby back to Screener Desk
	10 Steps from Screener Desk to Reception for Assessment Log
SCREENING	10 Steps from Reception back to Screener Desk
	10 Steps from Reception back to Screener Desk
	25 Steps from Screener Desk to Open Case Retrieval
	25 Steps from Open Case back to Screener Desk
	10 Steps from Screener Desk to Reception Bucket
ASSESSMENT	15 Steps to deliver file to ASW
	15 Steps from ASW to pick up client
	15 Steps from Lobby to ASW desk
	20 Steps from ASW desk to Copier / Printer

Figure 8.9   Counting steps

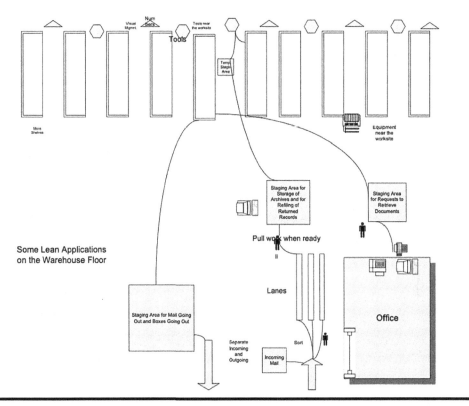

Figure 8.10 Archives floor plan

Figure 8.11 File buckets of each team's work to be done

Chapter 9

Pause
Putting It All Together

Gather All Information Pertaining to a Future Improved State

<u>Say in your own words:</u> The goal of this chapter is to fully develop our improvement ideas. These ideas need to be complete and robust and showing recommendations backed by supporting data.

Let's review...what do we know now? (The team will call out items that can be recorded on the flipchart.) *(If you need some prompts for the team, read aloud some of the Facilitation Deliverables at the end of each chapter. After this activity, the team will be surprised at the amount of work they have accomplished and what they have learned. Tape this flipchart page, Accomplishments, on the wall. This will help later in refining the PDSA forms.)*

Gather PDSA's and Sort Improvement Ideas

<u>Say in your own words:</u> There was a reason to fill out the PDSA forms throughout the workshop. We didn't want to miss any fleeting improvement ideas. These forms will be the basis for formalizing the final work of the team.

Could I have you split into two groups, please? Locate yourselves on either side of the room. One group (list group) will gather around the Accomplishments flipchart list and make notes of where each item in the list can be researched for further information. (Start with the workpaper notebook.) The other team (PDSA team) will help go through all the PDSA forms. *(Both groups will work together after they do their initial tasks. For example, a PDSA form may be incomplete and more research needs to be done. The PDSA team will go to the Accomplishments list group to help them.)*

<u>Say in your own words:</u> Let me guide the PDSA team to get you started. This is what you need to do: a) Read through all the PDSA forms. b) Forms that are not written clearly should be gleaned from the rest of the pile. Find out who wrote the form needing clarification. Amend the form.

<u>Sort PDSA forms and label by category</u>

c) Sort all of them into stacks according to the different categories of Smoothing Out the Process: coming in, going through, performing the work, and supports. Make sure you annotate the PDSA form with some marking that indicates its category. *(By this time, both groups will have finished their initial work. Bring the entire RPI team back together.)*

Develop Pilot Tests and Recommendations

(INSTRUCTIONS: With the different stacks of PDSA forms, divide the RPI team into four mini-groups, each group taking a stack of PDSA forms according to a category, e.g., "Coming in.")

<u>Say in your own words:</u> As you review these piles of PDSA forms, review what you have learned about improvements "coming in" and "going through," "performing the work" and "supports." Using that knowledge, see if anything can be added to the PDSA forms to enhance the improvement idea. (For example, in the "going through the process" category, is there a PDSA form on minimizing or eliminating batching?) Also estimate if any PDSA improvement recommendation can be implemented right away or

needs a pilot test first before it is rolled out to the rest of the organization. (This information will be helpful when we do the Impact/Difficulty Matrix.)

Say in your own words: Now we need to prepare to sort out all the PDSA forms into what is doable and what has the most impact. Put all the different categories in one pile, one stack on top of another. (Double-check that they have a distinguishing category notation on them.) They all need to be renumbered sequentially. Could I please have a volunteer do that?

Develop an Impact/Difficulty Matrix

(INSTRUCTIONS: Draw an outline of an Impact/Difficulty matrix on the flipchart from Figure 9.2.)

Say in your own words: This is an outline of an impact/difficulty matrix. We will discover that we can't do everything within 30 days, the threshold for testing or implementing improvements of an RPI. Or, we can't develop the improvement idea because it crosses too many functions. This means that it is too complex and merits further analysis. This Impact/Difficulty matrix is a way to figure out what to implement first, second, etc.

Say in your own words: Let me demonstrate with an example.

(INSTRUCTIONS: Go to the flipchart with the outline drawn of the matrix. Demonstrate how to look at the matrix, understanding the X and Y matrix and the quadrants. Verbally read out an improvement recommendation from one of the PDSA forms. Then, out loud, state your reasoning for choosing the level of impact and the level of difficulty. Take your hand and go to the matrix on the flipchart and "draw" the imaginary intersecting line and point to where the sticky note with the number should be placed. See if the rest of the group agrees.)

(What is important here is to verbally explain your decision...show the team your thought process so they can get a feel of how to do it themselves. It's a judgement call. The thing to consider with "difficult to implement" is to ask how long it would take to implement? And the thing to consider with "impact" is how much bang for the buck will the improvement garner?)

Now that I have demonstrated, you all need to complete the matrix. In new mini-groups, each take a 1/4 of the sequentially-numbered PSDA's, and determine where it should be placed on the matrix. Mark a sticky note with the PDSA form number and place it on the matrix.

(Let the different mini-groups work together to come to agreement. And as soon as agreement is reached, one person from each team can place the sticky notes on the matrix.)

<u>Say in your own words:</u> Now that we have completed this matrix, does anyone have questions or comments on the placement of the sticky notes? (Discuss.)

One last task is needed for completing this matrix. I need two volunteers to make a list of the sequence of implementation of the sticky notes on the matrix. The sequence of implementation is determined by where the sticky note is placed. Start with the sticky notes in the low difficulty/high impact quadrant. Then move on from there.

In order to report out to the sponsor, the improvement represented on the sticky note has to have a short name put to it. Will someone please give a "headline name" for each sticky note These will be used in our oral report-out?

Prepare Supporting Documentation for Report-Out

<u>Say in your own words:</u> In preparation for our report out, 1. we need to make sure we have completed action plans for the implementation of the improvements, 2. that we have a flowchart of the future process, and finally, 3. that we can report out cost savings due to the RPI.

<u>Say in your own words:</u> Everyone needs to be working at once on one of these three topics. Please select a topic. The action plans group will go to one side the room; the future state flowchart group to the other side. And the costing-out group will meet in the back of the room. I will meet with each group and get you started.

Developing Action Plans

(INSTRUCTIONS: Meet with action plans group. Instruct them to ask, "What needs to happen to realize this improvement?" and "If we did a pilot test, what did we learn from that test to put into an action plan?") *(Here is where you will get questions such as "How long should an implementation take?" As a reminder, the rule of thumb is: implementations should be completed during the workshop or as soon as possible after the workshop ends. If the initial implementation takes longer than 30 days, it's time to reassess.)*

Validating Open Position	Activities	Line Mgmt	Department Mgr (Dir/AP)	HR Representative	Department Mgr HR	Head of C&B*	HR Administration		
1	Review Position	AR	C						
2	Creat draft job description	AR	C						
3	Complete Staff requisition form	AR	C						
4	Approve Staff requisition form		AR						
5	Inform HR Representative	AR	I	I					
6	Organise Open Position Review meeting	A		R	I	I			
A	Decide unchanged/ changed/new	I	I	R	A				
7	Update final Documentation	C	C	R	A				
8	Elevate Final Documentation for approval	I	I	R	A				
9	Approve Request for Staff form	I		R	A				
10a	Accept Request form: Inform Line Mgr.	I		R	A				
10b	Adjust Request form: Send back in process	I		R	A	I			
10c	Reject Request form: Inform Line Mgr.	I	I	R	A				

R = Responsible (execute)
A = Accountable (Yes or No)
C = Consulted before
I = Informed After

Figure 9.1   Example: Financial Services Budgetary Process RPI Matrix

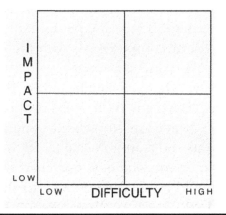

Figure 9.2   Impact/Difficulty Matrix

Say in your own words: Not only do dates need to go on an action plan, but also the people responsible for the action plan tasks. Here is a tool that will help you. It's a Responsible, Accountable, Consult, Inform (RACI) chart.

(INSTRUCTIONS: Hand out three documents from Appendix 9: Blank RACI Chart, HR Personnel Action Process, RACI Chart Instructions.)

Say in your own words: Look at your blank RACI chart. It should list steps in the action plan down the left side of the form and list names of

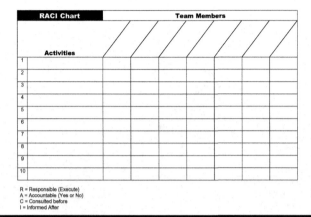

Figure 9.3   Blank RACI Chart

employees doing the task across the top. Please look at the other two handouts to help you fill out this chart.

Developing a Future State Map

(INSTRUCTIONS: Meet with the future state flowchart group.

Have a large piece of newsprint taped up on the wall to be used for the creation of a future state map. Beside it tape up the latest revised flowchart. And lastly, tape up the list of improvements with their title headlines (from the sticky notes) where everyone can see it.)

Ask the team, "What has changed significantly?","Has the whole flow of work been rearranged?", "Have any more steps dropped out?", "Have any new steps been added?", "Have any steps been combined?"

(INSTRUCTIONS: Facilitate the team in using sticky notes to build a new future-state improved flowchart. The new flowchart doesn't have to be super detailed, but it should be detailed enough to show the sponsor where the major changes are.)

(INSTRUCTIONS: Hand out "Three flowcharts, current state" and "One flowchart, future state" from Appendix 9.)

Say in your own words: Let's review these handouts. Look at the future state and think about how the team constructed it. They thought in terms of input (e.g., a submitted application), of process activities (e.g., what is done to that application), and of output (e.g., the document is stamped "accepted" or "rejected") and handed back to the applicant. Labelling the output on a sticky note, begins the development of the future state flowchart.

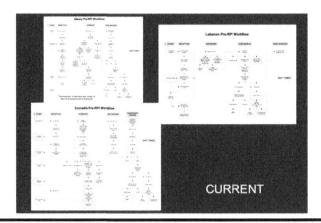

Figure 9.4   Example: Field Offices Client Application Process RPI-Current State Flowcharts

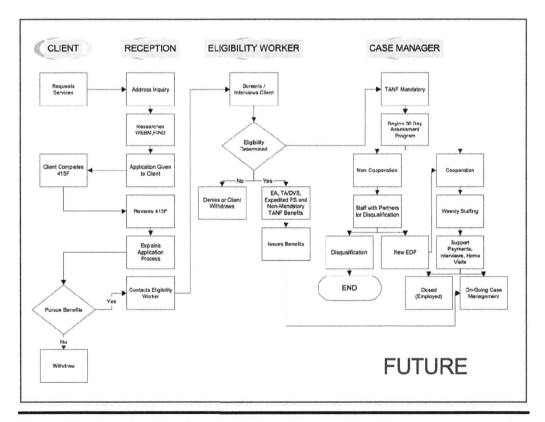

Figure 9.5   Example: RPI, Client Application Process-Future State

<u>Ask</u>, "what is the output?" *(There may be different answers from the team. They have to collaborate with each other to decide the wording of the output. If the mini-team gets stuck, lead them to think about what they know about the customers' expectations and needs. The team will eventually answer and name the output.)*

(INSTRUCTIONS: Put a sticky note with the name of the output on the blank piece of newsprint on the far right end of the paper. Then direct the mini-team to ask themselves, "What happens before this?" The team will respond with an activity in the process. This is written on a sticky note and placed to the left of the output. Have them ask the same question (what happens before this?) again and again, working through the workflow all the way to the left side of the paper to the first step in the process.

If needed, instruct the team to create new handoff and spaghetti charts and refer to the instructions in Appendix 2.)

Developing Before and After Costs

(INSTRUCTIONS: Meet with costing-out group.)

<u>Say in your own words to the group:</u> The presentation should include results of cost savings due to the RPI. Compare the cost of the process before the RPI to the costs post-RPI.

As guidance to get started: when figuring out costs, these should be exclusively the activities that represent work performed. Labor costs is a place to start. Think about how many people (including supervisors) work on that process, how long they work, and what is their hourly pay.)

(INSTRUCTIONS: Hand out: Costing Out Sheet, OHP RPI from Appendix 9.)

<u>Say in your own words:</u> This handout represents a model of costing out. This example is from the Oregon Health Plan Processing Center RPI. It is based on the current number of workers and their salaries for major parts of the process steps: Mail/Fax, Central Process, Eligibility, and Review.

Start at the ACTUAL box at top left. The numbers represent the volume of work for received applications for the month of July. You can see July in the box to the right. To the far-right top, you can see the box marked CALCULATIONS. This determines the amount of time that is available to do the work in weeks, days, and hours (per day).

Next, look at the middle of the page that has fields that list the different parts of the process starting with MAIL/FAX, then CENTRAL PROCESS, and then ELIGIBILITY, etc. The calculations displayed for each of these middle

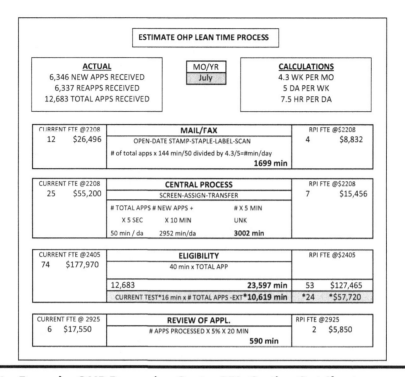

Figure 9.6   Example: OHP Processing Center RPI, Costing Out Sheet

boxes is the amount of time (in minutes) it takes to do the volume of work for the month of July. On the left is the box with the number of FTE's with corresponding salaries, before improvements. And to the right is the box of FTE multiplied by their salary from the improved process.

You total up each side and compare. The result is the savings due to the improved processes. Begin to collect your costing-out information by using this model example.

Documenting Post-RPI Metrics

Say in your own words: Post-RPI metrics compare the same kinds of measures used in the baseline, to measures taken after improvements have been implemented. Some improvements are implemented quicker than others, and their effects are ready for reporting. Other improvements can take longer to put in place. *(Ideally, improvements should be put in place during the workshop, but the gears of some organizations, including government, turn more slowly.)*

For the report-out date, for those measures that are not ready for reporting, the RPI team should extrapolate and report a good estimate. They should emphasize that these measures will be tracked bi-weekly or monthly after being put in place. At the end of each measuring milestone, there will be an indication of progress towards the target goals on the charter. The OHP RPI took measures quarterly. One of the measures was the number of days it took to process one application. From quarter to quarter, the days decreased as the improvements took hold. Another tracked measure was the dollar amount of overtime: this decreased significantly from quarter to quarter.

Documenting Specific Metrics

(INSTRUCTIONS: Hand out Travel Authorization Metrics from Appendix 9.)

Say in your own words: This handout shows a form that will provide a ready answer to anyone who questions the source of your data. This is an

• Specific information for each metric • Included in Final Report	**Metric #**	PHD01.1_4 (Assigned from PMO)
	Metric Label	Rework
	Definition	Percentage of travel authorizations requiring rework (e.g. documents/information is missing or inaccurate)
	Calculation	Number of requests returned to originator for correction divided by total requests in the same time period.
	Type:	☐ Workload ☐ Service/Cycle Time ■ Quality ☐ People Check the box that identifies the type of metric
	Source	OOS Travel Tracker
	Data owner	Travel Coordinator
	Data frequency	Weekly
	Baseline	75% (10/2/08 touch time survey)
	Target	25%
	Target timeline	3/1/09
	Benchmark utilized	None
	Metric start date	9/15/08 (OEPH Pilot); 11/10/08 (PHD-wide)

Figure 9.7   Example: Metrics from Travel Authorization Process RPI

example of a well-designed form that documents all aspects of taking measures. It's from the Agency Travel Authorization Process RPI. Note that the form gives a focus: reducing work. The corresponding baseline and target data are on the form copied from the charter.

The form clearly states the definition of the metric (percentage of travel authorizations requiring rework, e.g., documents/information is missing or inaccurate) and how it will be calculated (number of requests returned to originator for correction divided by total requests in the same time period). It gives the title of the person responsible for tracking (DOS Travel Tracker) and how often the measures will be taken (weekly).

Facilitator Develops a Draft Presentation Outline

(INSTRUCTIONS: write on the flipchart:

Scope and Goals.
Summary of results.
Current state: What's working; what's not working.
Analysis of what is not working.
Lean solutions.
Action plans.
Summary of before and after states (e.g., current vs future flowcharts, baseline metrics and target goals.))

<u>Say in your own words:</u> Here is a draft outline (not final) for the report-out presentation. I am going to read aloud some questions for you to consider in developing our final presentation outline in the next chapter.
(INSTRUCTIONS: Read aloud.
For the final outline, we need to ask, "What does the audience want to hear in 30 minutes?"

- Did the workshop solve the problem stated in the charter?
- Will the improvement recommendations meet the target goals?
- Is there anything radical that is recommended that the audience doesn't know about?
- Are there estimated money savings to be reported?)

List of Facilitation Deliverables

- Completed PDSA forms.

The Art of Facilitation: Unions

Unions are concerned that Lean improvements could cut jobs. But the intent of Lean is not to eliminate jobs, but rather streamline the flow of work to free up the capacity of employees working on steps that are not necessary, considered waste.

Most government workers have a much bigger job than they are able to do. Their work, in any given day, looks like a bowl of overflowing spaghetti. The management style is often crisis-management and workers play catch-up daily.

One of the benefits of Lean improvements, is that it frees up a worker's capacity by removing unnecessary activities in a process and reconfiguring the work flows. This waste and convoluted work paths add time and expense to a process. If workers are freed up, they can work on many tasks and planned, future projects, that before Lean, there was no time to work on them.

Appendix 9

HANDOUTS:

RACI Chart		Team Members						
	Activities							
1								
2								
3								
4								
5								
6								
7								
8								
9								
10								

R = Responsible (Execute)
A = Accountable (Yes or No)
C = Consulted before
I = Informed After

Figure 9.8 Blank RACI Chart

EXAMPLE: Human Resources RPI RACI Chart

Validating Open position	Activities	Line mgmt.	Dept. Mgr (DirVP)	HR Representative	Department Mgr HR	Head of Classification	HR Administration
1	Review position	AR	C				
2	Create draft job description	AR	C				
3	Complete staff requisition form	AR	C				
4	Inform HR representative		AR				
5	Organize Open Position Review meeting	AR	I	I			
6	Decide unchanged/changed/new	A		R	I	I	
7	Update final documentation	I	I	R	A		
8	Elevate final documentation for approval	C	C	R	A		
9	Approve request for staff form	I	I	R	A		
10a	Accept request format: inform Line Mgr.	I		R	A		
10b	Adjust request form: send back in process	I		R	A	I	
10c	Reject request form, inform Line Mgr.	I	I	R	A		

R = Responsible (execute)
A = Accountable (Yes or No)
C = Consulted before
I = Informed after

Figure 9.9   HR Personnel Action RPI RACI Chart

HAND OUT:- Instructions for RACI Chart

1. Place 'accountability' (A) and 'responsibility' (R) at the lowest feasible level

2. There can be only one accountability per activity (eliminate checkers checking the checkers)

3. Authority must accompany accountability

4. Minimize the number of 'consults' (C) and 'informs' (I)

5. All roles and responsibilities must be documented and communicated

6. First fill in the Rs –who does the work. Then fill in the A's –those with the ultimate authority.

7. Remember only one A per task.

8. A position can have both the A and the R

9. Try to place the A at the lowest reasonable level to minimize excessive sign-offs and levels of approval.

Figure 9.10   RACI Instructions

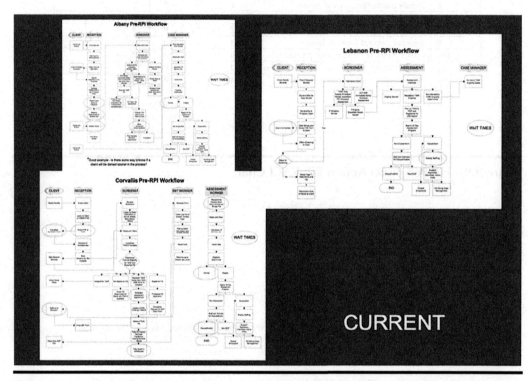

Figure 9.11 Three flowcharts, current state, Field Offices Client Application Process

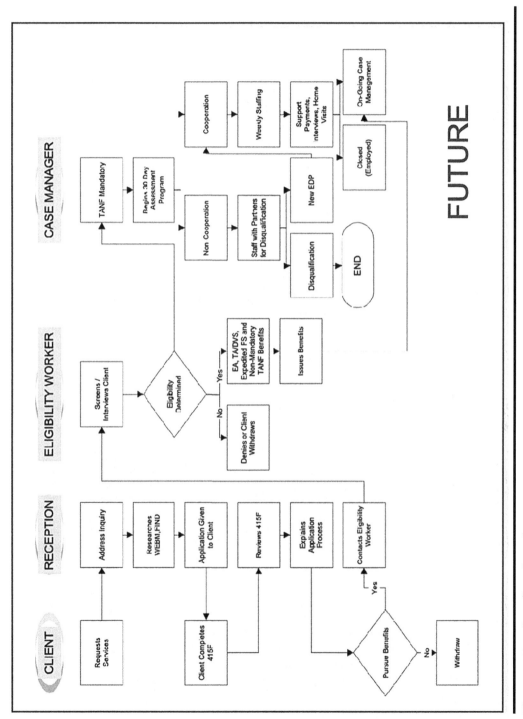

Figure 9.12 One flowchart future state

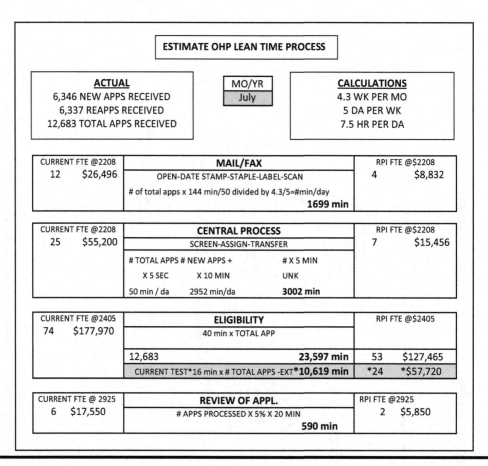

Figure 9.13   Costing out Calculation

- Specific information for each metric

- Included in Final Report

Metric #	PHD01.1_4 (Assigned from PMO)
Metric Label	Rework
Definition	Percentage of travel authorizations requiring rework (e.g. documents/information is missing or inaccurate)
Calculation	Number of requests returned to originator for correction divided by total requests in the same time period.
Type:	☐ Workload ☐ Service/Cycle Time ■ Quality ☐ People Check the box that identifies the type of metric
Source	OOS Travel Tracker
Data owner	Travel Coordinator
Data frequency	Weekly
Baseline	75% (10/2/08 touch time survey)
Target	25%
Target timeline	3/1/09
Benchmark utilized	None
Metric start date	9/15/08 (OEPH Pilot); 11/10/08 (PHD-wide)

Figure 9.14   Agency Travel Authorization RPI Metrics

Chapter 10

Report, Implementation Tracking, and Continuous Improvement

Part 1. Oral Report-Out, Written Report, and Dissemination

Prepare the Final Presentation Outline

(INSTRUCTIONS: Hand out Presentation Outline from Appendix 10, Part 1.)

Say in your own words: We ended Chapter 9 with a draft presentation outline. Now we need to finalize it. This handout is an example of a presentation outline from the Youth Authority Incident Resolution Process RPI. It lists the names of the presenters and the times allotted for their part. I ask for your feedback and input.

(INSTRUCTIONS: Have the team take out blank paper and write their input and suggestions for the final outline and note if they would like to present. Give them 10 minutes and then collect their suggestions.)

(As the facilitator, you are responsible for the final presentation outline. Considering all the input from the RPI team, you are going to have to boil down all the RPI work into salient points for the sponsor and other managers to hear within the short time allotted for the presentation.)

(INSTRUCTIONS: Develop a final presentation outline.)

Outline of Report-Out to RPI Sponsor, J.O., May 12, 4 pm.

The RPI Team: S. H., W. S., H. B., T. J., A. B., Paddy O'Brien

Agenda:

•5 min. Review of the charter, what was the charge to the RPI team? (Paddy)

•8 min. Summary (with bullets on a flip chart) of what the team concluded (T. or A.?) (What were the sticking points, where was the most vulnerability in the current process, etc.?) Basically, "where did we end up" before moving on to recommendations?

•15-20 min. These conclusions let to the following recommendations (W. and H.) (not too much detail...but try and group the recommendations in the following areas: timeliness (how can the current process be beneficial if it is so late?), assuring safety (and therefore preventing the 'writing of the check!), and to share learnings and share best resolutions and practices.

•5 min. and a quick overview of the action plan/Gaant chart (W.)

•10 min. Summary in anticipating J.'s concerns about safety and prevention for the next time the incident happens and learning opportunities and education. (S..."When we recommended....we addressed shared learnings....")

Figure 10.1 Presentation Outline, Youth Authority Incident Resolution Process RPI

Presentation Rehearsal

Say in your own words: Now I am going to ask some of you to formally present. For the rest of the team, you will help in preparing visuals, handouts, and creating a PowerPoint presentation.

(INSTRUCTIONS: Based on the outline, as the facilitator, select people from the RPI team to take on a part of the presentation. Add the names and times to the final outline. Make copies of the final outline; distribute to all team members.

Work with each presenter to write their own script. Remind them that improvement recommendations should be cited with the reasoning behind their development. Numerical data should support the recommendations. And visuals need to be included such as "before and after process maps," and "baseline data compared to estimated future data."

While they are working on their scripts, have them make a list of what supporting materials they will need to tell their part of the story. Use these lists when assigning work to the rest of the team.)

(INSTRUCTIONS: From what is needed for the presenters, the rest of the team can self-select to work on the following tasks: handouts, visuals,

PowerPoint presentations. Distribute ideas and suggestions that you have and help the different task groups get started. You will have to be the "liaison" between the presenters and the task groups to make sure what is needed, is developed. (Study the example of a PowerPoint Presentation in the Appendix 10, Part 1, Self-Study.))

After the details of each presentation are ready, have a rehearsal. You are watching for presenters to stay within their time limit. If they don't, review the script with the presenter. *(You are also paying attention to the comfort level of each presenter. Some may need more encouragement or coaching before the final report-out. Work with these individuals privately.)*

<u>Say in your own words:</u> Now that we have had a rehearsal, can you think of questions that will come up from the audience? Please, just call out a question and then we will discuss possible answers.

Oral Report Out

(INSTRUCTIONS: The RPI team makes their presentation starting at the designated time.)

(At this time, you, as the facilitator, are nowhere near the presenters. It is their show. You are standing in the back of the room while the presentation is being delivered.

Figure 10.2   Team reporting results

If you follow the outline for the presentation and you prepare and show a slide presentation, everything should run smoothly. Ideally, there should be few or no questions at the end. Remember, the discipline used in the workshop regarding the collection of enough data to validate an improvement idea and using the PDSA forms to test theories for improvement should give the audience confidence that the suggested improvements are worth implementing. And if there is any additional time, the team would be proud to tell their audience how they did it!)

(INSTRUCTIONS: As the team finishes their report out, you, as the facilitator, can come to the front of the room and communicate "next steps.")

<u>Say in your own words</u> to the audience attending the presentation: Three things will happen now. First, a draft report will be written. Often, when we compare what we hear about a subject and then read about that same subject, which tends to be more accurate. The draft written report is completed soon after the end of the workshop. It is distributed immediately to key persons for review.

The next thing that happens is establishing a tracking system that measures the progress of the improvement implementation and the results of that improvement over time. Last, but not least, what occurs is the merging of measures and results of RPI improvements into an organizational continuous improvement system which will have a physical or digital location to be continuously monitored.

Written Report and Dissemination

(As the facilitator, you are responsible for writing the report, getting it reviewed, and assuring its dissemination.

It is my experience the report "writes itself" if you do your writing bit by bit during the week of the workshop. In the evening of each day of the workshop, I record what happened during the day and examine each PDSA form that was submitted that day. This provides the start of a paper trail that makes it easy to pull the report together.)

(INSTRUCTIONS: Write the report as soon as you can after the workshop ends. (Make sure and refer to the Appendix 10, Part 1, Self-Study, Choosing a format for the report and read the following information for writing and dissemination.

The place to start your writing is to first review the outline of the oral report out presentation. Then review the contents of the Workpapers

The Workpapers' Notebook (Chapter 1) is the first resource for the writing of the report. The notebook should contain the following information that has been collected during the workshop:

1. Workshop Goals sheet.
2. All filled-out PDSA forms.
3. Calculation of TAKT time (if appropriate).
4. Work layout chart.
5. Annotated floor plan (location of staff, equipment).
6. Waste documentation documents.
7. Five Why's documentation.
8. Pareto Chart.
9. Flowchart revisions and future state.
10. Cycle time. Lead time.
11. Experiment data.
12. Pre-RPI data.
13. Time observations, footstep counts between workstations, handoff counts.
14. Documentation of best practices.
15. Analysis of leveling the workload.

Figure 10.3   Contents of the Workpapers from the workshop

Notebook and notes from each day of the workshop. Review the PDSA forms.

Write the report.

The review and delivery of the report:

Here are the steps for the review and delivery of the written draft report:

1. When the draft of the report is completed, cross-check any facts and figures to the Workpapers Notebook.
2. Make sure the draft is water-marked "DRAFT" on each page. Deliver it to the sponsor to review. The sponsor should review for accuracy. *(The sponsor may also want to have a manager or lead worker review the report. In such case, you will deliver a copy to them.)*
3. Once the report is reviewed, make sure you retrieve all draft copies. *(Why? The final report may be different than the drafts and you don't want any inaccurate or incomplete draft reports floating around.)* Make changes to the draft and finalize the report.
4. The sponsor will give you a list of the people who should get the final report. *(These should be managers and staff affected by the improved processes.)*

Appendix 10, Part 1

HANDOUTS:

Outline of Report-Out to RPI Sponsor, J.O., May 12, 4 pm.

The RPI Team: S. H., W. S., H. B., T. J., A. B., Paddy O'Brien

Agenda:

•5 min. Review of the charter, what was the charge to the RPI team? (Paddy)

•8 min. Summary (with bullets on a flip chart) of what the team concluded (T. or A.?) (What were the sticking points, where was the most vulnerability in the current process, etc.?) Basically, "where did we end up" before moving on to recommendations?

•15-20 min. These conclusions let to the following recommendations (W. and H.) (not too much detail…but try and group the recommendations in the following areas: timeliness (how can the current process be beneficial if it is so late?), assuring safety (and therefore preventing the 'writing of the check!), and to share learnings and share best resolutions and practices.

•5 min. and a quick overview of the action plan/Gaant chart (W.)

•10 min. Summary in anticipating J.'s concerns about safety and prevention for the next time the incident happens and learning opportunities and education. (S…."When we recommended….we addressed shared learnings….")

Figure 10.4   Presentation Outline, Youth Authority Incident Resolution Process RPI

SELF-STUDY: Aids for the presentation and format for final written report
Using a PowerPoint in the report out

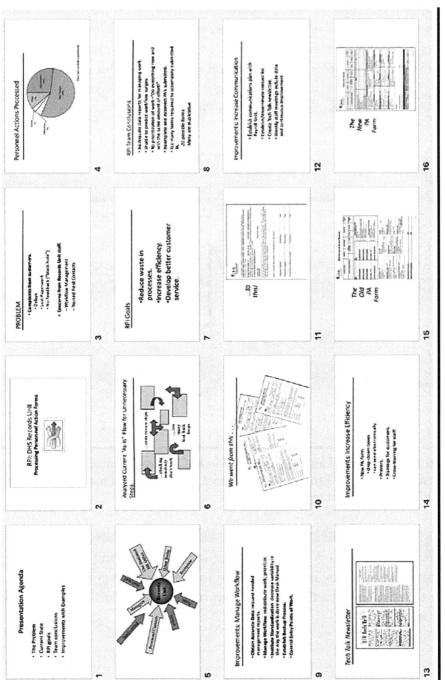

Figure 10.5 Human Resources Personnel Action Process RPI, Report out Presentation

Choose a format for the report. *(My RPI reports look like a format I used in previous jobs. I add appendices to my RPI reports, as evidence of the work done to support the improvement recommendations. However, I soon learned that many readers of this kind of report thought it was too long; they didn't have time to give it a thorough read. So, I changed it. I put a succinct Executive Summary up front, that gave the reader pertinent information quickly.)*

Here is a sample of written report formats.

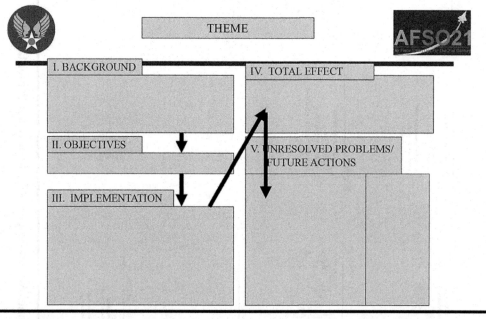

Figure 10.6 An example of an A-3 form used in the Air Force Smart Operations for the 21st Century (AFSO21) Process Improvement Program. Used for reporting the results of their improvement events

■ An example of an A-3 Report Format used in reporting results from improvement events in the Air Force Process Improvement Program. Note the similarity to the information on the PDSA forms used in this manual.

Problem Definition

Coordination and timeliness of preparing a workspace and computer access for a new employee is cumbersome and often times delayed. This results in lost productivity. This work shop is the second RPI done on this subject. (An RPI was completed on the Add, Move, and Delete (AMD) process in June, 2007 and resulted in a revised AMD form, a new HR Employee Checklist, a new Needs Assessment Form, and an official written procedure change to the-then current process.) AMD means the access to information (with a minimum amount of risk) to data systems, networks, intranets that must be in place for a new employee to start work the first day on the job! This 'first day preparation' also involves security clearances, the purchase of new computers and software, moving furniture, installing phones, and smooth processing of all personnel paperwork. Recently, an Information Security directive enforced an HR policy which required completion of a new employee criminal record check be completed and entered into the PPDB system before the access to systems be started. This process, housed in DHS Administrative Services continues to generate many complaints, especially from the field. These complaints resulted in a review of the entire process from recruitment for a vacancy to the arrival of the employee on the first day of work.

Baseline Data-subprocesses

Recruitment	9 steps	6 handoffs	3wkscycletime
Records	8	3	24 hrs.
AMD	14	2	31 days
CRU	5	2	2 d or 2 wks
Newcomputer	9	7	24 days
Furniture-HSB	3	2	7 days
Phones	5	2	24 days

Business Goals Metrics

Business Goals = Faster cycle time of all processes that contribute to the readiness of a new employee's computer access, environment, equipment and security clearances so that they can begin to work..

Metric =reduce cycle time 50%.
Improve quality
FTE Capacity
$ Saved

Deliverables

- *Implementation plan.*
- *Flow diagrams*
- *Lessons Learned-key categories*

Milestones

Recommendation steps. Report all for the Report Period

Description	Plan	Actual	Status
<major deliverable>			G
			Y
			R

Dependencies/Risks/Assumptions

Dependencies: Field offices, program/cluster offices, central offices including facilities, HR, OIS service Desk, OIS Asset Management, Telecommunications, PPDB, TIM, DHS Office of Information Security.

Risks: Appropriate access to information security must be assured for all employees affected by the AMD process.

Risk: Clarified roles of accountable managers or their delegates in authorization of approvals.

Staffing/Resources

- % Jeremy Emerson - Project Sponsor
- % Melody Riley - RPI Team Lead
-
- % <name> - <title>

Current Dashboard Status

Planned Action complete	X%	G	QA Followup Date met	
Schedule Variance	X%	Y	Business Transition (Is there going to be training;do you need a communication plan?	
Scope (?)		R	Infrastructure (new flowchart)	
Changes (?)			Resources (Leads on Recommendations)	

Figure 10.7 One-Page Report, New Employee Add, Modify, Delete Process RPI

- An example of a one-page report that includes a problem definition, baseline measures, and a whole monitoring system based on the dashboard developed with red, yellow, and green boxes to indicate the progress of the implementation of the action plan.

EXECUTIVE SUMMARY

In the 05-07 biennium, the use of an errant formula was found contained on the spreadsheet that depicted the allocation amounts to different AAA's. Due to the makeup of any Excel spreadsheet, formulas are hidden and the staff person merely sees the results of the formula, not the formula itself. The formula error was hidden in the spreadsheet for a long time and was not caught earlier, resulting in an overallocation of federal funds over two (2) biennia. Obviously, there is a need for checks and balances early in the process. Although this situation was an anomaly, SPD management took action and requested a Rapid Process Improvement Workshop (RPI). The RPI was chartered to determine the systemic problems of the Award Allocation Process and improve it or design a new process.

At the heart of this issue, is the accountability SPD has to the AAA's and the AAA's accountability to SPD. AAA's must be assured that the monies that they are getting through SPD are allocated appropriately and timely in order to plan for their programs with adequate staff and services. And conversely, SPD must be assured that monies are being spent the way intended and can report accurately to the federal government. There is much 'paper exchange' that goes on between SPD and the AAA's, i.e. letters of notification, allocation sheets, contracts/amendments. There is also much 'paper traffic' that goes on between SPD Program, DHS Budget and DHS Accounting. And lastly, there is the amount of information and documentation going from the AAA's to SPD: signed contracts, budget plan and budget expenditure sheet, and transfer notification.

The RPI Team set out to correct a broken process: the Award Allocation Process. In order to accomplish this, the team learned and applied Lean concepts that were carried out through the RPI (see pg. 25). They flowcharted all the relevant processes, learned about identifying 8 types of waste, understand the need for continuous flow as to not hold things up with batching, standardizing and leveling work flow, and most of all questioned the current process steps by asking, "Why do we do this step?"

There were four distinct areas of concern that they focused on:

- **Timely notification**...on all documents, when received, when sent, and when received again. For example, an Award Letter from AOA arrives in the SPD mail and can sit on someone's desk for days. This can back up the entire process. The RPI recommended improvement in removing this bottleneck at the point of entry of the process.

- **Allocation Integrity**

Figure 10.8 Excerpt from Report – Older Americans Act Allocation Process RPI

There needs to be integrity in the formula as well as the allocation model that is used in distributing monies to the AAA's. The formula is cumbersome, harder still to input further into a complex model. In addition, the RPI team had much discussion around equity of distribution as expressed by many AAA's, there was other discussion from the team whether equity should be replaced with "appropriateness" meaning that some sort of past performance of each AAA should be considered in a formula. Examining the end-of-year budgets and analysis of carry-over amounts might acknowledge an equitable distribution but perhaps not equitable spending.

- **Budgeted Allocation Timeline**
  Because the 'tail wags the dog', SPD must wait until Congress passes a budget that includes Older Americans Act monies before they can allocate monies to the AAA's. The Congress is supposed to do this in order to meet the beginning of the Federal Fiscal Year, Oct. 1. However, for the present and the near future, Congress will not make the Oct. 1 deadline and all beneficiaries of federal funds will operate on a "continuing resolution" which means you spend at the same level that you were budgeted for last year.

  So for the first few months of the federal fiscal year, the SPD budget submitted with increased need (base on allocation formula calculations) is rather useful. The dilemma for SPD is how to instruct the AAA's as to amount and spending of their budget. Basically, it has been "live on what you got last year" and as actual awards come in, SPD will allocate and disseminate as quickly as possible. What a nightmare for all involved...there were ten partial awards sent to SPD the last federal fiscal year. Ten times, the formula and model had to be recalculated (and do this all while coping with Federal Fiscal Year transactions that transverses to State Fiscal transactions (see pg. 22).

- And last, but not least, the **budget expenditure reporting** is overly documented and assumedly then over controlled. There were many reports that are submitted to the AAA's to show how they spend their monies. There are numerous copies made of these reports and they are dispatched to many DHS staff that analyze and review them. The team had to ultimately ask, "What is the intent of the submission and review of these forms? How come there are duplicate reviews and what is held up in the rest of the process due to this messy 'back and forth' of documents?

Figure 10.8 Excerpt from Report – Older Americans Act Allocation Process RPI (*Continued*).

- A formal report format with an executive summary followed by more details in the body of the report. This example includes a table of contents and a listing of the appendices in the back of the report.

Chapter 10, Part 2. Tracking System and Continuous Improvement

Develop RPI Tracking System for Implementation

(The end of an RPI means a shift in roles. You, as the facilitator, no longer facilitate a workshop. Now you take on an advisory role to the process sponsor and the responsible managers on how to track implementation of improvements.

The entire part of this chapter is addressed to you, in your new role as advisor and trainer. Study the chapter for background information and steps to follow when working with sponsors, managers and intact staff work groups.)

The oral report and the written report are complete. Action plans are included with the written report or sent as a separate file. These action plans were developed by the RPI team in Chapter 9.

Action plans need to tie to an implementation tracking system that displays the progress of improvements towards the RPI target goals. The results from the tracking system become part of the organization's continuous improvement system and are displayed on a visual board.

The purpose of a tracking system is not only to communicate progress of implementation, but to give management the information they need to tweak the improved process as it matures.

To start setting up a tracking system, you need to work with the appropriate manager who will be the one ultimately accountable for tracking implementations. How do you know an action step for an improvement is complete? (We made a prioritized list of implementing improvements from the Difficulty/Impact Matrix. Which gives us information on the sequence of improvements to be implemented.)

There is some measure that is taken that tells whether the action step is complete. That all has to be figured out by the manager. The manager will assign a staff person to be the actual data collector and the manager will determine the frequency of collection. The measure, and any calculations, will be clearly defined. Each improvement headline has an action plan attached to it with detailed steps. As one detailed step after another is completed, the improvement headline will be notated "partially complete" until all detailed steps are fully completed.

Figure 10.9 Example: Percentage of completion chart from Continuous Improvement Register, Contract Administration Work Group

What Does a Tracking System Look Like?

Here is an example of what a tracking system looks like at the detailed action plan level. You develop a chart with all the steps listed and place an oval shape (that is marked into four quadrants) next to each step. As progress is made in completing that step, the oval shape is filled in, quadrant by quadrant.

Here is another type of tracking form.

When all action steps are completed, then the improvement headline can be marked as completed.

What	Who	Target Date	Status	Comments/Concerns
1. Create Standard Justification Form 1293 paper format	Kaysie	9/9/2008		
*focus groups, etc. on paper format	Debbie	9/12/2008	Complete	
*Piloting (1week) .	Eric and Kaysie	9/15/2008	Complete	
*Transfer form to .net/electronic	Katie	TBA	In process	Jeff, Katie, Hilary and Debbie revewiewing tweaks made to PDF form.
2. Define Standard travel packet and create checklist				
	Kaysie	9/9/2008	Complete	
4. Send Delegation memo to Section Managers	Niki	9/15/2008		
*Pilot		9/12/2008	Complete	Pilot group is permanently moved to new process to continue exercising it and to maintain morale boost.
*Division-Wide Roll Out		11/3/2008	Complete	Process Implemented Division-wide on 11/3/08!

Figure 10.10   Action Plan, Agency Travel Authorization RPI

Establish a Continuous Improvement Framework with a Daily Management System (DMS)

(As noted earlier, the end of an RPI means a shift in roles. You, as the facilitator, no longer facilitate a workshop. You may be asked by the organization to advise and train on building a continuous improvement system.)

A continuous improvement system framework bridges the gap between the RPI accomplishments to the continuous monitoring of those RPI improvements. But the framework is more than this. It's a vehicle for making continuous improvements that don't require a week-long workshop; in fact, they can be made daily.

The framework encompasses a daily management system that organizes intact work groups, trains them in process improvement, and establishes a central location for tracking metrics, communicating, and sharing work.

Identifying Logical, Intact Work Groups

The establishment of the continuous improvement system framework starts with identifying intact workgroups. Each workgroup is defined ideally, as no more than nine people working in close proximity for most of the time. They have a "process" or "functional" connection pulling them together. This is known as an "intact" work group.

(INSTRUCTION: Consult with the management team to identify intact work groups.)

WHAT IF?...you see that your organization has some work teams but also a lot of sole practitioners? This is likely when you may have a lot of knowledge workers and they have few explicit routine processes. But even these sole workers see things that can be improved in their work.

What do you do then? Some organizations raise the viewing level of processes up to the value stream level. This would gather people who are working solo but on the same value stream to come together in huddles and developing a visual board. All in all, it's a judgement call by the organization. Some just leave the sole practitioners out of the DMS.

Figure 10.11   A challenge for facilitator

Work Groups Start Having Huddles

These intact work groups meet in "huddles." Huddles occur daily, last for 10 minutes, and are used to communicate, improve, and share work. (Huddles are like the daily editors' meetings at a newspaper. These editors decide what goes on the front page that day and who needs to be assigned to a developing story. These regular meetings provide a forum for needed communication and enables the editors to control the daily work, much like the benefits of huddles.) (INSTRUCTIONS: Hand out Daily Huddle Reminders from Appendix 10, Part 2.)

The intact work groups, now identified, need training in the whole composite of the Continuous Improvement System Framework. As the advisor to management, you can train the trainer or do the training yourself.

Set up a training schedule for each intact work group.

After completing the schedule, disseminate it and start organizing the rooms and materials needed. Send out an "invitation to training" email to each intact work group.

Schedule for implementing daily management improvement system

WEEK 1

- DMS orientation for staff and employees
- Agree on the role for manager, supervisors, team leads, etc.
- Identify logical intact work groups

WEEK 2

- DMS implementation begins
- Begin daily huddle meetings
- Design and display a Visual Display Board including existing metrics and post any RPI implementation schedule

WEEK 3

- Begin Continuous Improvement Action Sheets
- Identify focus metrics for each workgroup

Figure 10.12   Weekly Schedule for establishing daily management system

Huddles are the work teams' daily meetings held at a specific time and place, agreed to by the team. People stand, not sit, and the meeting time is limited to 10 minutes.

The first few huddles will be led by the trainer. Later, this role will go to one of the huddle members. With these first huddles, there is no agenda. The goal is to set a habit of meeting regularly and just have a place to communicate. Next, the team will build their own visual display board. This will be designated as the location where the team huddles. This is important because the team will be constantly interacting with what is displayed on the board.

Setting up a visual display

The visual display will be the anchor for the content of the huddles. It will include information that the work team will use on a daily basis such as huddle attendance and cross-training. (INSTRUCTIONS: Hand out Huddle Attendance Chart, Skills Versatility Chart from Appendix 10, Part 2.) Locate a large white board preferably on a rolling stand for the team's use. If no white board is available, find a large bulletin board or a large wall space covered in blank newsprint.

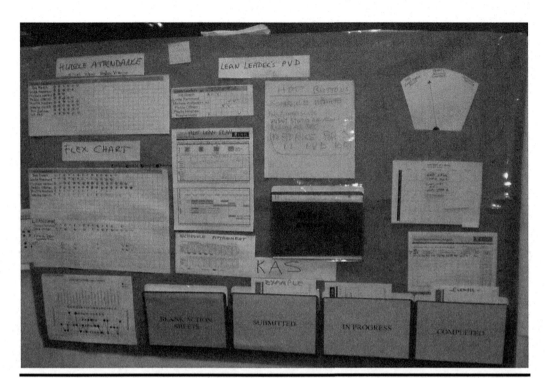

Figure 10.13   Example: Visual Display Board, Lean Leaders Work Group

Developing the visual display: the visual display is built one piece at a time.
Visual display item: Huddle Agenda

Build a basic huddle agenda. A more complete agenda can be developed when the visual display board is fully populated. This would include a run-through of Hot Topics, charts of metrics, staff attendance, skills matrix, action sheets, and selected work team performance metrics. The basic agenda would start like this: "let's start with hot topics." Then the facilitator would ask who wrote the specific hot topic and ask that person to share it with the group.

Visual display item: Hot Topics

Figure 10.14   Hot Topics

Put up a small whiteboard in the lower, middle part of the visual display and put a sign above it that says Hot Topics. (Remember to put up a dry erase marker attached to the board.)

The work team needs to agree on the criteria for what constitutes a hot topic (many times, this is important information from a management meeting, news article, legislative action, etc.).

Explain how the small whiteboard is used. (Anyone in the intact workgroup, can put topics on the small whiteboard as long as it is done before the huddle starts.) Whatever is written on the whiteboard will be addressed in the huddle.

Manage the continuous improvement action sheets

The action sheet system is the mechanism for getting suggestions for daily improvements in front of the huddle. (INSTRUCTIONS: Handout the blank Continuous Action Sheet from Appendix 10, Part 2.)

Figure 10.15   Folder system for improvement ideas

Explain that the action sheet system is made up of action forms used to communicate and convert process improvement suggestions into real change within employee work units.

On the visual board, tape or staple four different file folders (a different color for each folder is preferable). Mark them boldly: **blank**, **submitted**, **in-progress**, and **completed**.

Explain how the folder system works. When someone has an idea for an improvement, he/she takes a form from the **blank** folder, fills it out, and puts it in the **submitted** folder. During the huddle, the filled-out form is retrieved, assigned an action, and moved to the **in-progress** folder. When action is completed, the form is marked as such, and moved to the **completed** folder and recorded on the Continuous Improvement Register located on the visual board. (See Self-Study, Appendix 10, Part 2.)

(One of the overlooked challenges in using this system is this: not everyone knows how to articulate an improvement idea to go on the action sheet.)

To make sure the work group knows what to put on a blank action sheet, go back to basics. Improvement opportunities arise because there is some sort of waste in the process. If a team member learns to identify waste, such as an unnecessary step, this is the start of an improvement idea.

(INSTRUCTIONS: Hand out the list of wastes from Appendix 10, Part 2.)

Go through the list of wastes and clarify. Instruct the work group: when they recognize waste in their workplace, they can start their action sheet by writing the kind of waste they see and where the waste is located. When that is complete, they can ask themselves, "why is the waste there?" This should lead them to an improvement idea.

Let me read aloud, "When to write down an idea." (Read contents of Figure 10.16.)

When should I write down my idea?

1. When I see a mistake being made in my work area.
2. When the problem happens.
3. When something you do every day makes you think there is a better way to get the job done.

Figure 10.16 When to write down an idea. Questions for the workgroup

Train how to facilitate the action sheets in the huddle

Take a pause in putting up more items on the visual board and use the time to train in how the action sheet system works.

The huddle has started; the facilitator is going through the agenda and gets to the item "action sheets."

First, the facilitator reads one of the submitted forms and says aloud, "Carl has put in a suggestion for this..." (and the facilitator continues to read the entire improvement idea).

Next, the facilitator decides on how to handle the suggestion through the following options:

- the facilitator will handle it or...
- the facilitator will ask if anyone would like to handle it or...
- the facilitator can assign it to someone or...
- if the facilitator has some doubt, discuss it with the team to possibly turn the idea down. The facilitator would could start by saying, "It's too big for the team and the idea may need an RPI."

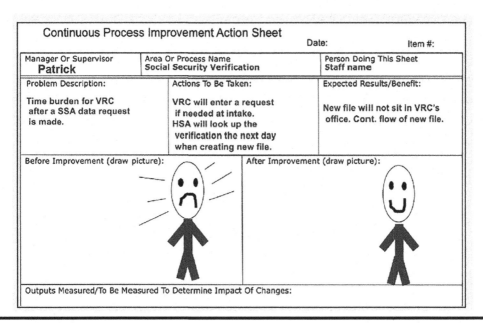

Figure 10.17   Completed CI Action Sheet, Vocational Rehabilitation Office work team. A good example of an idea for an improvement

Lastly, the facilitator writes the assigned person's name on the action sheet. Then puts the sheet into the **in-progress** folder. The person has 48 hours to report back to the huddle with a plan of how the idea will be implemented. The plan is recorded on the action sheet and moved to the **complete** file.

Helping the work group select their metrics

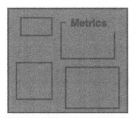

Figure 10.18   See Appendix 10, Part 2 Self-Study Team Measures

Small improvement ideas, implemented continuously, can have an incremental improvement effect on the whole picture. It's important for the work group to monitor their own progress towards success. These measures have to "mean something" to the work team. Start by asking the group, "How do you know you are successful?"

Here is where process thinking comes in. Does the work team have a customer (can be a person, another work group, or another organization) they can identify? What does the customer receive from the work team? And if the customer is satisfied, then the work team can count that as success. Customer satisfaction can be measured and tracked. Some work groups track timeliness and others track mistakes or incompleteness. Collecting and displaying this data can be assigned to someone on the work team. This data can be displayed on graphs and put up on the visual display. Occasionally, some huddle time will be used to discuss trends from the charts.

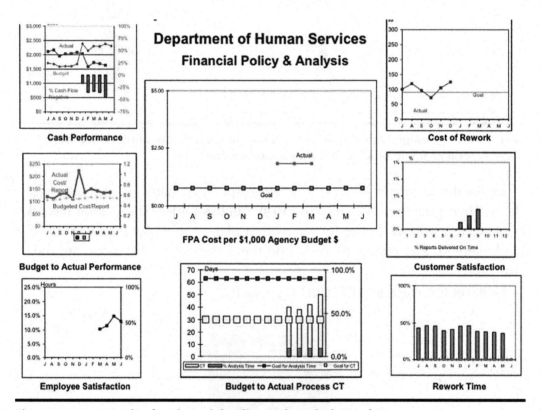

Figure 10.19   Metrics for Financial Policy and Analysis Work Team

List of Facilitation Deliverables

- Presentation documents.
- Training materials for continuous improvement system framework.
- All documents to be put on the display board.
- Documentation of intact workgroups measures and metrics and their monitoring.

Appendix 10, Part 2

HANDOUTS:

DAILY HUDDLE REMINDERS

1. On most days, a regular huddle facilitator is assigned, usually a team lead and supervisor.

2. Keep it relevant. Stand-up meetings. Only 10 minutes.

3. Start on time; end on time.

4. Decide what the huddle agenda should be for that day.

5. Don't solve problems. Just identify.

6. Discuss metrics. Always include if tracking daily or weekly data.

Figure 10.20   Daily Huddle Reminders

Huddle Attendance Visual Display

Employee Name	DATE									
	○	○	○	○	○	○	○	○	○	○
	○	○	○	○	○	○	○	○	○	○
	○	○	○	○	○	○	○	○	○	○
	○	○	○	○	○	○	○	○	○	○
	○	○	○	○	○	○	○	○	○	○
	○	○	○	○	○	○	○	○	○	○

Figure 10.21   Huddle Attendance Chart

Skills Versatility Visual Display

Team Member	Skills of tools or tasks								%
	⊕	⊕	⊕	⊕	⊕	⊕	⊕	⊕	
	⊕	⊕	⊕	⊕	⊕	⊕	⊕	⊕	
	⊕	⊕	⊕	⊕	⊕	⊕	⊕	⊕	
	⊕	⊕	⊕	⊕	⊕	⊕	⊕	⊕	
	⊕	⊕	⊕	⊕	⊕	⊕	⊕	⊕	
Task Flexibility									
Task Coverage									

Circle Quad = 25% skill level

Figure 10.22   Skills Versatility Chart

Type of Waste	Examples	Location
Overproducing/overprocessing-More effort than is required. Difficult to see and uncover.		
Correction-redoing or reworking and returns.		
Inventory-excess or unneeded stock, files, supplies, idle work in process, in-box.		
Waiting Time-Delays and queues of all types. Interruptions-stoppage in work activity due to some external factor.		
Searching Time – Time spent looking for info, people, supplies, equip. Unnecessary work movements.		
Transport/travel-Multiple handling steps and needles movement of people, material, info.		
Space-Storage of unneeded items, etc. Excess space required due to inefficient process flow.		
Complexity – complex process flows. Product choices that confuse customers. Organizational boundaries that are inefficient.		
Travel/transport- Movement by a performer from his or her workstation to another place.		
Rework-Behavior to a process a product/component to salvage a defective unit or part. (Re dos, fix ups, returns).		

Figure 10.23   List of wastes

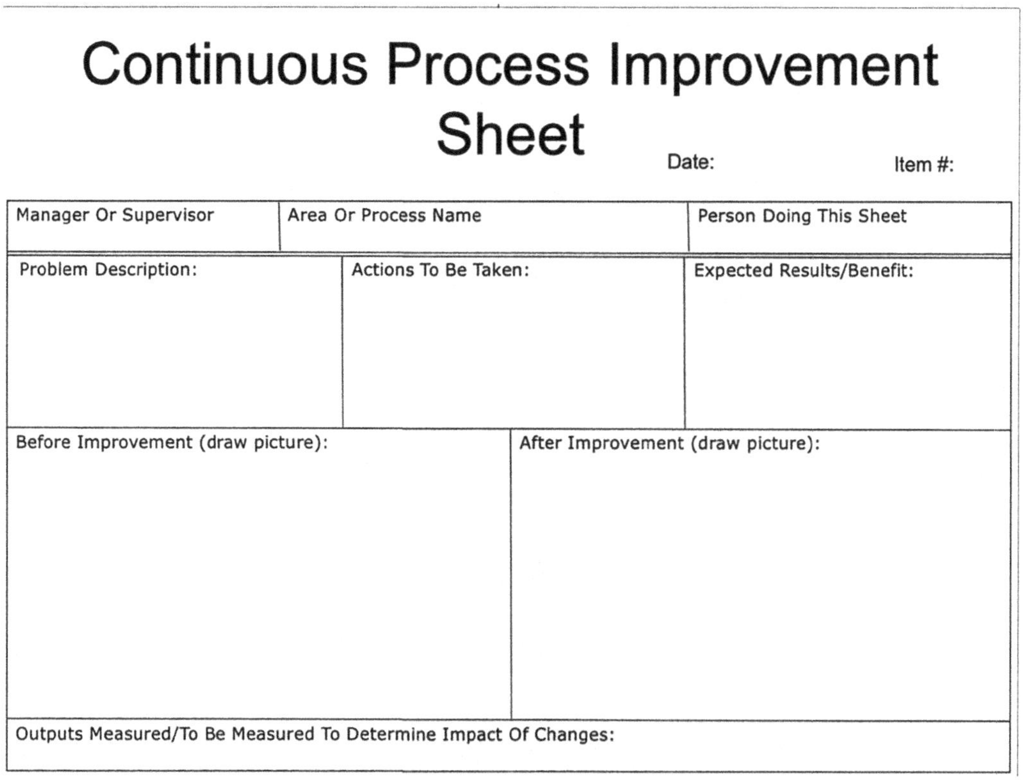

Continuous Process Improvement Sheet

Date: _____   Item #: _____

Manager Or Supervisor	Area Or Process Name	Person Doing This Sheet
Problem Description:	Actions To Be Taken:	Expected Results/Benefit:

Before Improvement (draw picture):	After Improvement (draw picture):

Outputs Measured/To Be Measured To Determine Impact Of Changes:

Figure 10.24   Continuous Improvement Sheet blank form

SELF-STUDY: More detail on setting up the visual display board
<u>Displaying daily huddle attendance</u>

DAILY HUDDLE ATTENDANCE

Employee Name	3/5	3/6	3/7	3/8	3/9	3/10	3/11	3/12	3/13	3/14
Larry	●	●	(PD)	●	●	○	○	●	(v)	(v)
Bob	●	●	●	●	●	○	○	●	○	○
Curly	●	●	●	●	●	○	○	●	○	○
Moe	(v)	(v)	●	●	●	○	○	●	○	(PD)
Sally	●	●	●	(PD)	○	○	○	●	○	○
Roberta	●	●	●	●	●	○	○	●	○	○

● Present   ○ Excused Absence/Late   ● Unexcused Absence   PD = Personal Day   V = Planned Vacation

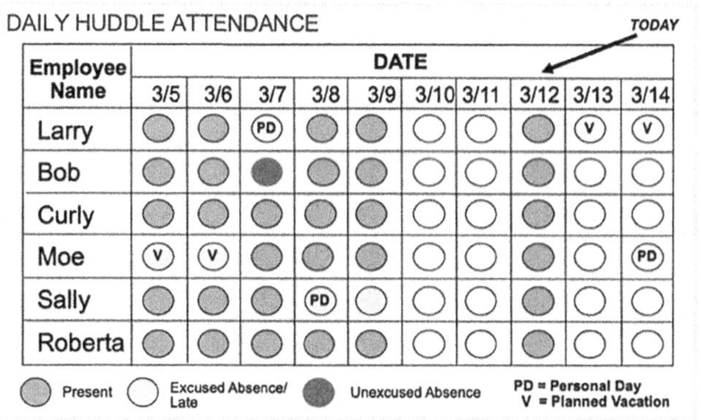

Figure 10.25   Filled-in Daily Huddle Attendance

Why is it necessary to record huddle attendance? Recording this helps make the huddle a habit and it also lets the team know who is in the office that day.

Make up a form for attendance. Ask the team to develop the form they want and assign someone to manage it. This form is one example. It provides more detail than the team may want. Putting checks and "x's" for each name under each day may be sufficient.

Displaying workgroup schedule

Figure 10.26 Work group quarterly/yearly schedule

This is the organization/team schedule. Include known "out-of-office" times, such as vacations, trainings, personal days, meetings, etc.

Displaying a skills versatility matrix

	Not Familiar With It		Familiar		Training Needed		Do It Without Help		Can Teach It

Process or Task

Team Member	Excel	Word	PowerPoint	Writing	Appeals	Negotiate	DSU Lead	%
Larry	●	●	●	●	●	●	●	96%
Bob	●	◑	○	○	○	◑	◑	32%
Moe	●	○	○	◑	●	●	◑	57%
Sally	●	◑	○	●	◑	●	●	68%
Task Flexibility	100%	50%	25%	56%	50%	81%	81%	63%
Task Coverage	9/9	1/9	2/9	3/9	4/9	6/9	2/9	

Figure 10.27   Filled-out Skills Matrix

A skills versatility matrix, sometimes called a "Flex Chart", is about worker flexibility. This means the worker is skilled at performing a variety of tasks. The development of this chart takes about a month. The first thing you do is list all the skills that are needed to do the tasks of the work. You use this form. List about seven skills on one axis and staff names on the other. Where the skills and staff names cross each other, a circle will be filled in by quadrants. Each staff person determines their level of competence with each skill by filling in a certain number of quadrants.

(Question: Why is a skills matrix good for a work group?
Answer: because the group's tasks can be managed better since they can share the tasks whenever there is an increased demand in a critical function. Also, if someone is absent, others can fill in.
Question: But what does this chart do for worker motivation?
Answer: Recognition for those who strive to be proficient in more than one job or task.)

Displaying the continuous improvement register

This register is placed to the right of the "completed" folder on the board. And is used to track all the improvements made from using the action sheets.

Continuous Improvement Register

Manager Or Supervisor: WHITNEY PARKER
Area Or Process Name: CONTRACT ADMINISTRATION
Date:
Person Responsible For This Sheet: NICOLE DUPREE
Page: of

Item #	Problem Description:	Corrective Action	Person Accountable	Date Due	Percent Complete
1	CHECKS w/ TOO ERRORS REQUIRE LENGTHY SYSTEM CHECKS	Talk w/ of Brenda for Picture of any flaws in CHECKs Talk w/s re: BOBBH	BARBARA	7/30	
2	OFF-CYCLE REQUESTS period clarify what to cust. finance	Talk w/ cust. finance and come about setting up POINTERS cust finance	BARBARA	7/31	
3	CHECK reconciliation for hour, to be created for each instance	Create form w/ check off from Disputes for Barkley	BARBARA	7/31	
4	RIGHT ACCOUNT the acct too long to approve	Develop template and capacity agreement Discuss w/ Q Kelly	NICOLE	8/1	
5	APPLY DISPUTE notification Denny Reap letter that should only those those items of disk clients		NICOLE	8/3/01	
6	wholesale/retailing incorrect contact info for government	For VA contracts — notify wholes re: 2011 contracts	BARBARA	8/31/01	
7	non-dollars manually fast-track impact for finance	Discontinue process wholesalers do not place non-pw until do add'l $	BARBARA	7/31	
8	moving manual manually processing changes				
9	Automatic Contract to recession - fast Fix?				
10	Reformatting HELP w/ula spreadsheet to import to CAPS	Create access QRY to convert all check for import	BARBARA	8/3	

Figure 10.28 Filled out Continuous Improvement Register

Displaying team metrics to put on visual board

The work team will want to answer the question: how do we measure our work? Here are some examples to get started:

①Workload	②Service/cycle time

• Incoming cases per week
  – Cases closed per week
• Cases closed per week per FTE
• Average processing time to complete a task
  (e.g., interview length, visit length)
• Utilization (e.g., percentage of interview
  slots filled)
• Other tasks completed per week (e.g., visits
  per week)
	• Total end-to-end cycle time broken down by
	  – within control/not in control
	  – Major milestones
	• Cycle time for specific "trouble" process by
	  – process step
	  – within control, not in control
	  – cause of variability (e.g., FTE, source,
	    destination)
	• Percentage of cases pended/delayed

③Quality	④People

• Percentage of errors (from audit)
• Percentage of cases needing rework
• Percentage of cases needing rework by
  root cause
• Client satisfaction (survey)
	• Attendance split by
	  – Present / absent
	  – worker type (e.g., HSS1, HSS3)
	• FTE satisfaction
	• Lean "behavior"

Figure 10.29   Examples of typical measures and metrics – these should cover 70–80% of what you need

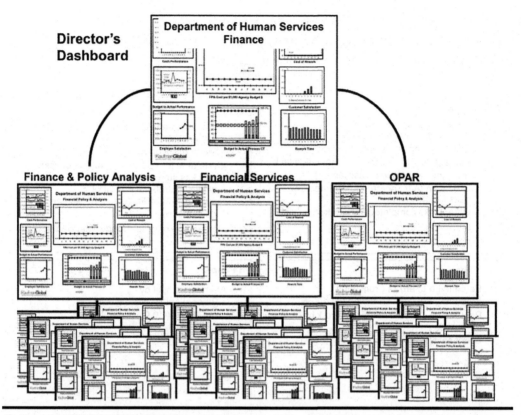

Figure 10.30   Example: Metrics, Financial Services RPI. Note: Intact Work Group measures on the bottom roll up to management units (finance and policy, etc.) and those roll up to the Director's Dashboard

Chapter 11

The End of the Story

This is the end of the manual. How did we do? AND what did we do?

As you study and glean the Lean concepts and methods in this guide, you will see a clear decision has been made to <u>not</u> stray from the integrity of Lean principles. What this means is that general problem-solving is not necessarily Lean problem-solving. An improved process is always a good thing, but a process improved using Lean methods is endurable. Why? Because Lean processes are measured and can be continuously improved.

The table of contents of the manual follows the standard agenda of a Rapid Process Improvement (RPI) workshop. This comes in handy so that if you are in the middle of an RPI, you can quickly get information. The index at the end of the book allows you to research a number of topics, tools, and techniques. Each chapter has a list of facilitation deliverables to use as a check on yourself.

Let me summarize the path we took, with all its intricate layers.

Chapter 1

We started by laying the foundation for the workshop. Key to this chapter is communicating to the RPI team their role in administrative tasks. The foundation included preparing the RPI team mentally for the work ahead.

This chapter, and all the ones following, spelled out what you, as the facilitator, could do. It also spelled out what you could communicate or teach to the RPI team, whether it meant demonstrating how to use a tool or giving the team a frame of reference by reading aloud a real-life example from a completed RPI workshop. *(In addition, to be of more help, there are notes inserted in the middle of text in* **italics** *to relay lessons learned on a particular point.)* One of the most important administrative tools introduced to the team is the Plan, Do, Study, Act (PDSA) method. All team members are asked to fill out a PDSA form for the purpose of tracking any improvement idea they may have, no matter how undeveloped it is. Ideas come up throughout the workshop and they should not be lost.

The most important part of this chapter is to focus on developing the paradigm of process thinking. I encourage all facilitators to be comfortable in their own ability to think in terms of process because you will be calling on this paradigm many times during a workshop.

Chapter 2

Like any other problem-solving technique, the second chapter is to help the RPI team understand the problem in front of them, i.e., understanding the current state. Unlike more traditional problem-solving techniques, this chapter incorporates many references and historical documents that can shed light on the problem. This includes pertinent legislation or policy that governs the processes. *(This is just a small part of what you had to learn to be prepared to facilitate this RPI. Equipping yourself with such knowledge puts you on a more level playing field with the sponsor and the RPI team.)*

Although you will find little Lean lingo used in this guide, this chapter makes the concept of Gemba become real. (Gemba is a Japanese term meaning "the actual place.") The RPI team gets their first taste of seeing a process at work, moving as outsiders to observe others' work spaces. They go through the gnarly exercise of translating "what they see" and putting it into a picture, i.e., a flowchart or process map.

Chapter 3

Lean improvement is more about action rather than studying the problem. The underlining theory of effective RPI workshops is that discovery of "what to improve" and "how to improve it" does not take place around a conference table but where the process work is being done. The RPI team conducts tests, gathers information, and interviews the staff out in the workplace.

In Chapter 3, we see something different than the more traditional path of RPI workshops. In this chapter, the team is "doing" improvements. They focus on one type of improvement, removing the "dead wood" from the process, much like pruning a tree. This chapter guides the team to get to the discovery of waste by seeing it in context. The team looks at the process and asks prescribed questions about the steps and flow. Their goal, in this first set of improvements, is to improve the speed in the process without making mistakes. For the process to be Lean, it must rid itself of unnecessary steps that impede efficiency.

Chapter 4

This next chapter is uniquely written for this manual. From my experience, it is important to take a pause in the workshop. Why? Because of the RPI team. The team has learned a lot more about the problem they are dealing with since they were first introduced to the workshop charter, which spelled out "the terms of the workshop." As the facilitator, you do not want to leave the team wondering whether they can accomplish the goals set in the charter. The charter is reviewed here by the team with the sponsor and if any changes need to be made, they are made.

Also, in this chapter, the team will be taught the option of ending the workshop at this point. They may come to the conclusion that the work they have done thus far, fulfills the goals of the sponsor. Although the final decision is left up to the sponsor, the team is shown a matrix about different paths and protocols a workshop can take. (They learn it all depends on the complexity of the problem and whether the solution is readily known.)

Underlying each one of the matrix protocols is the requirement to collect data to support whatever solution is recommended, no matter how obvious it is. This emphasizes another principle of Lean workshops: the importance of collecting enough data to support a team's improvement recommendation. Lean draws from eminent quality experts, W. Edwards Deming and Walter Shewhart (who gifted us with the theory of PDSA), to ensure that scientific theory is applied in a workshop.

The next three chapters of the manual can all be grouped together as the second set of improvements. In Chapter 3, the team makes improvements by focusing on the steps of the process, but now the team is focusing on the "flow". These next chapters are grouped into "Smoothing Out the

Process." When a process is smoothed out, it flows seamlessly; there are no delays.

Chapter 5

This chapter is designed to smooth out the process at the beginning, where the work comes in. There are many kinds of improvements that can be made about the work coming in. For example, one can separate the work into simple or complex cases or fast-track some of the incoming work into an express lane. This chapter comes back to an emphasis on data, the importance of which is stressed throughout the manual: collect enough data to support improvement ideas. The first example shown in this chapter is the collection of trend data that tracked how much work, what kind of work, and when the work enters the process. This knowledge helps management anticipate surges in work and rearrange the work force.

Chapter 6

This chapter transitions from "incoming" to "going through." One of the pieces of data the team collected early on (in Chapter 2) was noting the time in between steps. This is a clue in that longer times between some steps compared to the other steps, the longer times indicate a delay and need for further analysis.

Remember the emphasis on process thinking in Chapter 1? Here is where process thinking enters again. The team depends on you, as the facilitator, to take what seems an abstract concept, like "flow," and make it "real." Using a metaphor of what is the opposite, helps. For example, show a picture of a clogged freeway that shows "no flow." This chapter goes on to explain the many Lean concepts and techniques to apply in developing an improvement recommendation.

Push or pull, Kanban, and balancing the workload are in this chapter. Of particular note is the unique challenge of determining takt time which is the number that sets the "pace" of the process. Takt is very easy to determine when you have rote, routine processes as you do in a manufacturing factory. But it is almost impossible to determine in a lot of service delivery organizations like governments and non-profits. The Art of Facilitation write-up in this chapter is particularly interesting as it highlights a new kind of worker, the knowledge worker, who goes through many steps of a process in their heads. Therefore these steps are not readily explicit for analysis and improvement.

Chapter 7

This last chapter on smoothing the flow focuses on HOW the work is performed. In order for there to be a smooth flow of the process, variation in tasks has to be minimized or totally eliminated. The obvious kind of variation is that two people, doing the same job, can go about performing their tasks very differently from each other. The ramifications of variation are dire. As soon as customers start comparing notes with each other and realize a different level of time and completeness from one output to another, the organization will lose customers. The customers of government services can't easily walk away (because there is no alternative source of service), but they can complain to their legislators. This can hurt the reputation of the government agency; complaints have a potential to snowball. Some agencies have suffered budget cuts because legislators felt that they weren't performing.

This chapter is mainly about standardization to minimize variation. The important Lean concept here is that the people who perform the work develop the standards.

Chapter 8

Often missed, and only considered as an afterthought, are the supports to a process such as materials, equipment, and environment that are foundational to Lean improvement recommendations. The example of forms is used to show the RPI team how an improvement is made. In one RPI, there were many different forms for one process, and some of the fields of one form were duplicates of fields on other forms. The improvement was to eliminate duplication. Forms were decreased from 39 to 8!

These supports were outlined in a handout that stated what questions to ask about material, equipment, and environment in order to elucidate where improvements could be made.

Chapter 9

Like Chapter 4, this is a "pause" chapter. This, and the next chapter and addendum switch emphasis on roles. The chapters are full of direct tasks that you, as the facilitator, have to take on.

This chapter answers the question, "How do we pull all the learnings and work done by the RPI team together to form a cohesive oral report-out presentation and written report?" This is where each chapter's facilitation deliverables and all the PDSA forms are helpful.

The deliverables provide the background for the RPI and data on the problem. These include visuals necessary to a good presentation like "before" and "after" flowcharts. The deliverables also include data collected at the beginning of the RPI that will be compared to data from the completed improvements.

And where do the PDSA forms fit in? They are the foundation to developing full and complete improvement recommendations. The team is taught how to sort the forms and put them into manageable order. Then they are able to rank them based on what is possible to implement first, second, etc., while having the most impact.

And lastly, you have developed an agenda for the report out presentation and you have selected team members to take a part. Your role, as the facilitator, is to disappear into the background during the presentation. Following the report-out, a formal RPI report is written by you, and delivered to the sponsor and responsible managers as quickly as possible after the workshop ends.

Chapter 10

This chapter includes the setting up of monitoring systems for tracking the progress of improvements. Your role, as facilitator, is different now. No longer will you be directly facilitating a workshop, but you will become a consultant and trainer regarding setting up a tracking system. You will be very instrumental in guiding the sponsor and process managers on what to track, how to track, and when to report on progress.

This chapter is also the segue into developing a continuous improvement system for the organization. There are many models for this, but the one used in this manual is to teach managers and staff to empower intact work teams to obtain knowledge and tools to continuously improve their work.

This is accomplished by providing training to the intact work groups on developing a daily practice of meeting in small "huddles". When the huddles become routine, the workgroup then develops a large visual display. The display is also to be used to track the implementation of improvements from the recently completed RPI workshop.

Chapter 11

You are reading this. It is a continuous improvement chapter of the manual itself.

Addendum

This is what you, as the facilitator, have to do to prepare for the RPI Workshop.

Many weeks before the RPI start date, a list of tasks are outlined week by week. For example, the tasks listed like this: labelled, "six week before the workshop" and "the one week before the workshop" and "the day of the workshop."

Addendum
Prep Work for the RPI

6 Weeks Prior to Event

a) Meet with the organization's management team.

   The organization has decided to do a Rapid Process Improvement Workshop. They invite you to a management meeting to discuss what is involved. Your role is to listen carefully and ask questions. The questions you ask are to clarify that the problem they want to be addressed is a "process problem" and not something else, such as a personnel problem. And you want to make sure that they understand what is involved in an RPI roles and responsibilities. *(Suggestion for what to discuss in the management meeting:*

   - *Is the problem being presented a process problem?*
   - *Clarify exactly what to improve.*
   - *Can the problem's solution be implemented in a reasonable amount of time?*
   - *Can a few people implement the entire solution within a week without pushback?*
   - *Are metrics in place and readily available?*
   - *Choosing the method for improvement.)*

   Take time to create a small PowerPoint presentation that will explain what happens in an RPI. Make sure they understand that, as managers and supervisors, they need to allow selected staff to serve on the RPI team. They need to know that they will have to prepare for coverage of the day jobs of the RPI team for the days the workshop is held. During this meeting with managers, ask them to choose a sponsor of the workshop. This person is someone who has the authority to adopt the recommendations and implement the changes. In addition, during the workshop, the sponsor must be able to remove obstacles the RPI team encounters. The sponsor will also be the voice of the RPI workshop to answer questions from anyone on the staff. *(Remember, staff who are not on the RPI team will be wondering what this RPI team is up to. They will be asking if this team is going to make changes affecting them and their jobs. It is important that the "goings on" of the RPI team be transparent. The sponsor will figure out how transparency can be communicated to the rest of the staff.)*

b) Select a date for the beginning and the end of the workshop. Consult with appropriate managers and the sponsor to decide a day to begin the workshop. Depending on the complexity of the process(es), decide how long the workshop should be, varying from 1 to 5 consecutive days in a week. Then decide on the end date of the workshop. While researching the date for the workshop, you, as the facilitator should research calendars of other events, or conferences or holidays that may interfere with the day you have selected. Advise the managers and sponsor. Make sure and send out a "save the date" notice to those people who need to attend the Report-Out.

4–5 Weeks Before 1st Day of Workshop

a) Create a timeline for the prep work.

Use whatever tool works. A "work breakdown structure" can start listing key tasks which can be organized by date due. This does not need to be an elaborate project plan. It can be as simple as putting the first day of the workshop on a sticky note on a wall, then writing and placing tasks on sticky notes below it. The next step is to rearrange the tasks on the wall in order of what needs to be done first, second, etc. And then the last step is to determine who is involved in the tasks. Filling out a Responsibilities, Accountability, Consult, and Inform (RACI) chart can be useful here.

b) Schedule rooms for the workshop.

In my experience, meeting rooms are in demand. As soon as you know the dates of the workshop, try to schedule rooms that you will need during an RPI. I found that I need a big room or a couple of small rooms, as I periodically break up the team into smaller groups. *(As a rule, rooms to hold the event should be very close to where the organization's work is being performed. The original intent of proximity to the workplace is that it is easier for the workshop team to observe the process in action and easily collect information or other data that are needed during the event.)*

c) Clarify roles of sponsor, process owner, facilitator, and workshop team.

Sponsor:

- defines the mission of the event.
- ensures availability of appropriate team resources.
- ardent supporter of the event; clears barriers.
- accountable for presenting and selling event recommendations to others.
- ensures all appropriate communication is taking place.
- kicks off the event and actively monitors the event on a daily basis.
- attends the report out at the conclusion of the event.

Process owner:

- develops scope and objectives to put on the charter.
- identifies potential workshop team members and passes on to facilitat.
- champions the activities of the team.
- provides content knowledge.
- obtains additional resources as needed for specific tasks.
- develops any required documents and approves the final report in conjunction with the sponsor and facilitator.

Facilitator:

- Decides on the final list of team members and provides detailed information on the RPI process to all team members.
- delivers all required training.
- provides guidance on and/or lead logistics and planning.
- finalizes agenda and continually tracks activities against agenda.
- makes mid-stream corrections as needed to ensure optimal results.
- ensures that the team has required momentum to complete the RPI.
- assists in the creation of all RPI deliverables.
- utilizes Lean office tools and techniques to drive the RPI process.
- facilitates report-out.
- provides consultation after the event to facilitate implementation.

d) Create a communication plan.

Communication plan. A communication plan is essential. These are the following communication bridges that should be considered in your plan: facilitator to sponsor, facilitator to staff, sponsor/manager to staff.

Facilitator to sponsor: communication daily. The facilitator should report to the sponsor the day's activities and potential improvement recommendations. *(The sponsor should have no surprises at the end of the workshop.)* Part of this daily communication is to ask the sponsor for any help needed by the team, e.g., removing obstacles. The facilitator may need to help the sponsor in making early presentations to the staff.

Facilitator to staff (staff who are not on the RPI team): communication daily. At the end of the day, the facilitator should write on a flipchart (that is displayed outside the team room) the team's activities for the day. *(A caution here is that you do not want write any change ideas that have not been fully developed. Remember, there is still much work to be done to test improvement ideas. However, you can list activities for that day on a display outside the RPI team room; invite the rest of the staff put up sticky notes with comments and questions that can be addressed the next day in the workshop.)*

Sponsor or process owner to the whole staff: Communication when necessary. The owner should communicate to all staff to give them information of what is going on with the RPI. Send an email periodically during the RPI and the few weeks after the RPI is completed.

e) Start drafting a charter.

The sponsor and the process owner must agree on the format and the wording in the draft charter. There are many templates available for charter development. (See Addendum Appendix.)

The facilitator reviews and makes recommendations for changes based on facilitation needs.

The sponsor and process owner acknowledge that a revised charter is possible based on RPI team suggestions.

f) Identify potential workshop team members and select the team.

There are many factors to consider when selecting an RPI team. Should staff be asked to volunteer or should they be selected? What are the most important criteria for selecting team members? Should there be a specified makeup of the team? And who makes the final decision?

The team should be made up of members who have some knowledge about the process problem. They can be either working closely with it, tangential to it, or only work periodically with it. Some teams have included a manager or even a "customer" of the process. Prior to the selection, review the charter and ask "who can best serve on the team to reach the charter goals?" *(Make sure that you, as the facilitator, know enough about the system and process to include all the players in the pool of potential team members.)*

Before final selection, contact the supervisors of the proposed RPI team members to get permission for their staff to sit on the team. Supply them with dates their staff will be needed and reasons they were selected. The supervisor needs to be alerted that the team may need to spend a few extra hours outside of the workshop times. Before the workshop starts, the team will need to attend a ½ day of training.

Contacting the supervisors should be done by the sponsor with follow-up from the facilitator. *(As the facilitator, you do have veto power on any potential team member that is suggested to you. I have nixed some team member candidates because the person exhibited a lack of openness and unwillingness to learn new things. This kind of person is very different than a skeptic. Skeptics on the team can play an invaluable devil's advocate role.)*

(How big should the team be? This can vary, but management principles define that a span of control for one leader is 8–10.)

g) To collect preliminary data and information (baseline data, preliminary flowchart of the problem process(es).)

Data or metrics of the process need to be collected prior to holding an event to establish a baseline measurement. Some of these data may already exist, while others may need to be created. Ask the sponsor to see if a couple of staff can assist in gathering this information. Here are examples of what to gather about the process:

- # of errors.
- % of time devoted to rework.
- cycle time.
- quantity of outputs.
- number of people involved in process.
- background information that would help in understanding the organization and its processes.

h) As the facilitator, take this time to reassess your own competencies. Before the workshop begins, refresh yourself and retool on these topics:

- Have a thorough knowledge of elements of a "process."
- Data: Kinds of data, how to collect and how to analyze.
- Knowledge of the effect of change.
- Navigate a workshop course.
- Lean strategies and tools.
- Make changes to the workshop agenda after monitoring the progress of the team.
- Know when to check in with the sponsor.
- How detailed a flowchart should be.
- How deep the root cause discovery should be.
- Study the legislation, important policies, and audit reports of the organization.

3 Weeks Prior to the Event

a) Finalize the list of RPI Team participants; send welcome letter.
   After the team is selected, you need to send a formal invitation and a welcome memo. The example that follows is from an RPI conducted at the Oregon Youth Authority.
b) Send a reminder about dates and locations of RPI events (pretraining for team, kick off meeting, and workshop duration) to: team members, sponsor, process owner, and appropriate supervisors.
c) Continue to collect and analyze preliminary data.
d) As appropriate, schedule in-person meetings with key staff. *(There may be times that a sponsor would like you to talk to someone who will be instrumental in the success of the workshop, such as the research staff or the IT help desk. By you explaining the workshop pathway, they can envision where they can fit in and be of help to you. You may need them along the way, and it is better to give them a "head's up" before the workshop.)*
e) Develop preliminary process map/flowchart of the specific process (es). You, as the facilitator need to take the lead in this task. The sponsor can pave the way with workers you may need to observe and interview.

From: C.M.   Feb.6, 2015
To: H.B., E.F.,T.G., A.B.,W.S.,S. H.
Subject: Invitation to a workshop

I would like to invite you to participate in a rapid improvement workshop to address concerns about the Critical Incident Review process. We are going to focus on the corrective action plans part of the process.

You have been invited because of your intimate knowledge of this process. We will meet for two consecutive two days to rapidly identify and fix the workflow problems dealing with the corrective action part of our process.

The Workshop will take place on March 18, 19. We will start at 8:30 and finish each day about 4 pm. On March 18, we will be meeting in the Santiam Room and then on March 19 in the Rogue Room. Both are located in Central Office.

Let me explain the theory of this type of workshop. It is used to focus on a workflow and improve it by taking out unnecessary steps and ensuring that there are no lags in the flow. The scope is intended to be laser-focused so that improvements can be made in a matter of days, not months. We can look at this as an incremental improvement. We can come back again for another workshop and do some other improvements.

A little explanation about roles: I am the sponsor which means I have the authority to take all your recommendations and act on them. H.B. will be our team lead and he can answer any procedural questions. He will be working with our facilitator, Paddy O'Brien, who is working with us to apply Lean in OYA. And of course, our Deputy Director, has a keen interest in this topic and will be kept informed as to our progress.

In your role as a team member, you are expected to be fully present those two days. If there is any reason you cannot do this, please let me or H. know right away. Paddy is also available and can be reached at any time paddy.obrien@oya.state.or.us.

Figure A.1   Example: Welcome to team. Youth Authority Incident Resolution Process RPI – The welcome memo spells out their role and what they can expect.

1–2 Weeks Prior to the Event

a) Finalize RPI Agenda.
   This facilitation manual gives you a good outline for an agenda. An agenda can be affected by how much work has been done before the RPI and whether or not this event needs to be one day or five days.
b) Confirm participants: distribute charter statement and agenda to participants and executive management team.
c) Send out "Three Questions Form" to the RPI Team.
   About 10 days before the start of the workshop, I ask the process owner and the sponsor to allow me to be the sole person to communicate with the team about the workshop. I want to establish trust with the team and have them look to me for the leadership of the RPI. One of the things that I do is that I send a memo to each team member and ask them to answer three questions before the workshop: 1. What do you see? 2. What's the problem? 3. What do you think the solution is?

(I assure them that their answers are confidential and come just to me.)

What this question and answer technique accomplishes, is that it allows the team to let off a little steam before the RPI even starts. And, as the facilitator, I get an idea of what is on their minds. This informs me as to the direction I will take in facilitating and setting the final workshop agenda.

d) Finalize preliminary current state process flowchart: transfer to large paper (e.g., brown paper roll, print the smaller version using a plotter printer, or put up a sticky wall. (A sticky wall is a plain plastic tablecloth that has been completely covered in spray glue on one side. It is easy to put up half sheets of 8x10 paper to represent process steps.)

e) Meet with process owner and sponsor to review final agenda and charter.

f) Touch base with sponsor: review key talking points.

The sponsor comes to speak to the team on Day 1 and you will help prepare the sponsor to cover the following points:

- Sponsor welcomes them and tells them what they should expect (paraphrasing the charter).
- Sponsor assures the team that whatever they recommend, as far as improvements, will be strongly considered, and most likely implemented with the right supporting data.
- Sponsor tells the team how much their time and work are appreciated and adds that a letter of commendation will go into their personnel file.

g) Create and print contents for background packets for all RPI team members for Day 1 of the workshop.

List of materials in background packets

- RPI agenda.
- charter.
- excerpt from Ways and Means presentation that includes this process.
- flowchart and other charts.
- pertinent laws or policies that affect the process.
- preliminary data collected about the process.
- organization chart.
- findings from any audits or evaluation reports.

h) Deliver 3-hour training to team on what is an RPI and what are Lean Tools? However you design the training, the following PowerPoint slides should help you. The #1 slide gives the team an overview of what an RPI event entails.

i) Make sure that all flipchart stands and flipchart pads of paper are ordered to be put into the rooms prior to the first day of the workshop. Make sure that enough tables and chairs are ordered for the room(s) and specifications of how to be arranged. *(I prefer setting up the team around a big table so the team can all see each other. Or, I set several small tables and they can sit where ever they like.)*

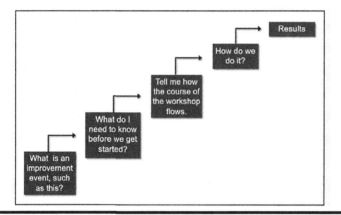

Figure A.2 #1 slide. Overview of an RPI

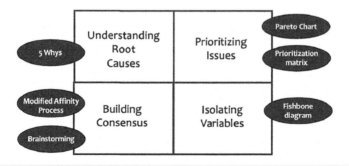

Figure A.3 #2 slide. Lean Tools and Quality Tools – The #2 slide spells out some Lean tools and Quality tools. Demonstrate some of these tools. One tool they must learn is "flowcharting/process mapping."

1 Day Prior to the Event

a) Ensure equipment is in working order.
   There is nothing that is more important than assuring the computer, the projector, the videos, and the speakers are all turned on and working right. Check the day before and again on the first day of the workshop. Have the IT technician's number handy.
b) Set up room, if possible.
c) Ensure all documents are printed and team background packets are put together.
d) Touch base with sponsor and team lead for any last-minute questions.
e) Prepare "RPI in a Box."
   "RPI in a Box" is all the supplies that you and the team will need during the workshop.

Get a large grocery box. Think about what you, as the facilitator, need during the workshop. Think about what the team will need. Make a list. Put everything in the box and make sure it is brought to the team room.

Day of the Event

a) Arrive: At least 2 hours before event. Dress professionally but casual. Be relaxed.
b) Room set-up: Ensure tables and chairs are set up the way requested. Place name placards at seats. Put two file trays in the middle of the

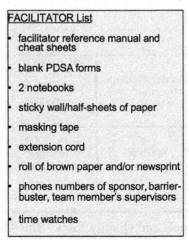

FACILITATOR List

- facilitator reference manual and cheat sheets
- blank PDSA forms
- 2 notebooks
- sticky wall/half-sheets of paper
- masking tape
- extension cord
- roll of brown paper and/or newsprint
- phones numbers of sponsor, barrier-buster, team member's supervisors
- time watches

Figure A.4   Facilitator list for RPI in a Box

```
TEAM List

• pens, pencils, notepads,
  tape, staplers, paperclips,
  Post-its

• flip chart paper and stands

• Sharpies and dry-erase
  board pens

• Rulers, flowchart template
  stencils

• Memory Jogger books

• a couple of laptops

• printer

• calculators
```

Figure A.5   Team list for RPI in a Box

team table. One is for blank PDSA forms and the other is for filled-out PDSA forms. As the facilitator, you will be the custodian of the forms and collect them at the end of each day to review them and put them in a PDSA file. The file will be kept where anyone can access it. In addition, you will need a large three-ring notebook labeled "Workpapers". This should also be kept in your custody but anyone can access it. Put up any posters on the wall that you may refer to, like the "Rules of the Workshop." Make sure there are enough flipchart stands and flipchart pads of paper. Have a big roll of newsprint ready.

- Roles and Responsibilities: If there is more than one trainer or facilitator, make sure roles are clearly defined and communicated between trainers/facilitators.
- Sponsor should be ready and prepped on what to say.
- Snacks: nice to have.

Appendix

PROJECT NAME:	Include an **Action Verb** (What we want to do) + **Noun** (What do we want to impact or improve?) "Reduce the number of days for new employee onboarding"		
DATE SUBMITTED:			
OPPORTUNITY STATEMENT: (Why is this important to the organization)	• What is occurring, what is happening, what "pain" are we or our customers experiencing? What is wrong or not working? • When did this problem start? How long has it been going on? • Where does it occur? • How much, or what is the extent or magnitude of the problem?		
TARGETED OUTCOMES: (Informed by visioning process and interviews)	• What are the **specific** outcomes we expect? "Reduce number of days by 50%" • What metrics will this project impact?		
STAKEHOLDERS AND RESOURCES:	**Names and Roles**		
Executive Sponsor	The person who is accountable for the success (results) of the project.		
Lean Project Leader:	The day-to-day leader of the effort (solution).		
Steering Committee:	Provides oversight, guidance to project. Participates in vision phase.		
Core Team Members:	Try to keep team to 6 team members. Make sure all process steps are represented by people who do the work.		
Extended Team Members:	SMEs or stakeholders who provide expertise, data or insight		
Champion/Mentor:	Lean Expert who will coach and mentor the project leader		
CUSTOMER GROUPS: (Note key segments here)	Who are the customers of this project? Who will be impacted by the project?		
PROJECT METRIC(S):	**Primary**	**Secondary**	**Consequential**
(Typical metrics include impact on quality, speed, and cost)	Typically lagging metrics that measure process outcomes and performance to customer requirements.	Input or process metrics (leading) Impacts that may be the result of the project but may not be project metrics.	Measure possible unintended and intended consequences.
SCOPE LIMITATIONS:	**In Scope**		**Out of Scope**
(Where are the boundaries?)	Start and End steps in the process. Which divisions are included?		What is not included?

Figure A.6   Example: Charter template, Lean Colorado. Charter Template – There are many templates available for charter development. On this page is an example from the State of Colorado. It is an excellent tool. In every field of the form, there are instructions for what should be written into each field.

Index

Page numbers in *italics* refers figures

Q

quality, 189
quality leaders, 103
quality tools, 207

R

reapplication reviewed, 91, 92, 97
Receipting Process RPI, 55
receptionists, 93, 106, 117–118, 129
recommendations, 148–149
Registered Nurse (RN), *91*, 91–92
report, 163–173, 196–197
  handouts, 164, 168
  oral, 163–166
  self-study (oral presentation and final report), 168–173
  written, 166–167
reputation, 195
resolution, 3, 11–12, 164, 168, 205
responsibility attribute matrix, 123, 129
Responsible, Accountable, Consult, Inform (RACI) chart, 151, 152, 158–159, 200
  instructions, 150, 157
ReVelle, Jack B., 14, 27
rework, 13, 45, 56, 63, 66, 76, 96, 103, 156, 184, 203
robust RPI, 71
room-scheduling (for RPI workshop), 200–201
root cause analysis, 68–62, 72, 79, 204, 207
routine, 6, 124, 197
routine processes, 108–110, 176, 194
RPI (Rapid Process Improvement) in Box
  facilitator list, 208
  team list, 209
RPI manual (this book)
  agenda of standard RPI workshop, 191, 205
  continuous improvement chapter, 196–197
  creation of, 1
  organization of, 1
  handouts, 5
  how to use, 2
  PDSA forms, 170
  point of departure, 1
  purpose of, 1
  RPI workshops successfully completed (list), 3

"smoothing out flow" chapters, 193–194
supports, 131
workshop pauses, 193; *see also* self-study
RPI team, 74, 191–196, 206
  composition, 199
  formal invitation, 204, 205
  morale, 71
  selection, 202–203
  size, 203
  training, 204, 207
  transparency, 200
RPI tracking system, 173–175
RPI workshop agenda, 191, 205–206
RPI workshop pauses, 71–84, 147–162, 193–194, 196
RPI workshop preparation work, 199–210
  charter template, 210
  day of event, 208–209
  one day prior, 208
  1–2 weeks prior, 205–208
  3–4 weeks prior, 204–205
  4–5 weeks prior, 200–204
  six weeks prior, 199–200
RPI workshops
  clarification of roles, 201
  duration, 5, 204
  foundation-laying, 5–27
  overview, 207
  possible alteration, 62–63, 71
  roles and responsibilities, 209
  successfully completed (list), 3
  termination option, 193
  underlying theory, 192
  words of welcome, 5

S

scientific method, 17
scope, 11, 80, 83, 210
searching time, 184
second walk-through (process to be improved), 29, 33–36
  data analysis, 36–40
  handouts, 33–36, 45
  instructions, 33–34, 45
  materials needed, 33

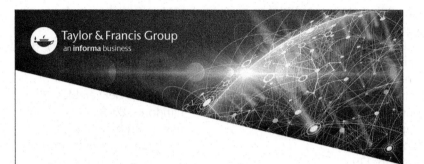

Printed in the United States
by Baker & Taylor Publisher Services